EXtraordiNaRy KIDS

EXtraordiNaRy KIDS

CHERI FULLER AND LOUISE TUCKER JONES
FOREWORD BY JONI EARECKSON TADA

PUBLISHING
Colorado Springs, Colorado

EXTRAORDINARY KIDS
Copyright © 1997 by Cheri Fuller and Louise Tucker Jones. All rights reserved. International
copyright secured.

Library of Congress Cataloging-in-Publication Data
Fuller, Cheri.
    Extraordinary kids/Cheri Fuller and Louise Tucker Jones.
      p. cm.
    ISBN 1-56179-558-5
1. Parents of handicapped children.   2. Parents of handicapped children—religious life.
3. Handicapped children.   4. Sick children. I. Jones, Louise Tucker. II. Title.
    HQ759.913.F85 1997
    649'. 151—dc21   97-21678
                                                       CIP

Published by Focus on the Family Publishing, Colorado Springs, CO 80995.

Unless otherwise noted, Scripture quotations are from the HOLY BIBLE, NEW INTERNA-
TIONAL VERSION ®. Copyright © 1973, 1978, 1984 by the International Bible Society.
Used by permission of Zondervan Publishing House. All rights reserved. Quotations labeled TLB
are from *The Living Bible*, © 1971. Used by permission of Tyndale House Publishers, Inc.,
Wheaton, IL 60189. All rights reserved. Quotations labeled *The Message* are from *The Message:
The New Testament in Contemporary English*, by Eugene H. Peterson, © 1993 by NavPress. Used
by permission. All rights reserved. Quotations labeled KJV are from the King James Version.
Quotations labeled NASB are from the *New American Standard Bible*, ©1960, 1963, 1968, 1971,
1973, 1975, and 1977 by The Lockman Foundation. Used by permission.

The authors are represented by the literary agency of Alive Communications, 1465 Kelly
Johnson Blvd., Suite 320, Colorado Springs, CO 80920.

Editor: Larry K. Weeden
Front cover design: Candi Park D'Agnese
Front cover photo: Tim O'Hara Photography, Inc.
Extraordinary cover models (left to right): Josiah D. Cisneros; Sara McHenry, Down syndrome;
Rebecca Anne Brant, spine muscular atrophy (SMA); Jeff Retting, deaf; and John E. Lusty,
Down syndrome.

Printed in the United States of America

97 98 99 00 01 02/10 9 8 7 6 5 4 3 2 1

To our son Jay. You have taught me more about loving Jesus, your neighbor, and your enemy than any preacher or teacher I ever sat under. You've given me more joy and laughter than I ever dreamed possible, and you've added a depth to my heart and soul that comes only through the fire. I love you more than life itself, and I pray you will always be blessed with as much happiness as you have given us.

Louise Tucker Jones

To my dear nieces: Judy, Natalie, and Eve. You three are champions in life and an inspiration to me.

Cheri Fuller

Contents

Acknowledgments

The love, patience, and contributions of many people have made this book possible. We are extremely grateful to all the parents of challenged children who shared their hearts and stories with us. And to all who contributed their thoughts and encouraged us, we thank you. A special round of applause goes to Valerie Campbell, Martha Little, Pam Whitley, Donna Johnson, Barbara Lumpkin, Louise Stewart, Pat Whitworth, and the Homemakers' Class. Your prayer support and wise counsel are greatly appreciated.

A sincere thank you to Focus on the Family Publishing, and especially to our editor, Larry Weeden, for his patience and editorial skills. To our agent, Greg Johnson, at Alive Communications, many thanks for your encouragement, promotion, and support of this project. To Mary Bowersox, thank you for keeping some routine in Jay's life during this writing.

Most of all we thank our husbands, Carl Jones and Holmes Fuller, for their love, patience, and even our meals when we worked through dinner. God has truly blessed us with their wonderful love over these many years—nearly 60 years of marriage between us. A very special thank you to Carl, who transported manuscripts back and forth for months without ever complaining.

To our children, we offer accolades of love for their patience and sweet spirits. Thank you, Jay, for allowing us to use your life as an example for so many people to see. And to Aaron, thank you for sharing your heart.

Foreword

A friend of mine, Gloria Hawley, fell into deep anguish over the prognosis of her daughter's illness. Little Laura had already suffered greatly from the degenerative nerve disease she had been born with, and now the doctor's forecast included more problems. Gloria, like any mother, wished she could take away her daughter's pain. She vacillated between times of sorrow and outbursts of anger.

Gloria left her daughter's bedside one night and cried out, "God, it's not fair! You've never had to watch Your child suffer or 'go without' or have friends turn their backs on Him!" With that, she clasped her hand over her mouth. God certainly *did* watch His child suffer: His one and only child. And, like any parent, He probably wished that He could take away His Son's pain. Yet God endured the pain—because God so loved the world.

That fact alone changed Gloria. She could finally bear the pain of her daughter's "going without" because God had borne the pain of His own child. This meant His strength and empathy were tailor-made for Gloria. She could take heart that God was by her side, giving her the most amazing parent support group ever devised. It made all the difference in the world to this mother of a special-needs child.

This incredible parent support group spreads far beyond God and Gloria. It includes Cheri Fuller and Louise Tucker Jones. It includes the stories of moms and dads in this special book you hold in your hands. Most of all, it includes you.

Your child may not be a "Laura" with a degenerative nerve

disease and a poor medical prognosis, but the issues surrounding the disability of your son or daughter are no less urgent, no
less critical. Your child may have cystic fibrosis, muscular dystrophy, or Down syndrome. He may be visually impaired. She
may be in a wheelchair, paralyzed from an automobile accident. Whether your child is autistic or dealing with attention
deficit disorder, you're probably like my friend Gloria—tena-
cious and intrepid, bold and bulldogish. You, friend, have
"screwed up your courage to the sticking place," as Shakespeare
would say. And whether that sticking place is in the hospital
waiting room, an IEP meeting, or the local social security
office, you are your child's best defender.

And you have help.

Extraordinary Kids has been written expressly for you.
Because for all your zeal, if you lack knowledge, you are only
operating at half speed. This book, written by two moms who
have "been there," is stuffed with practical advice for you.
Extraordinary Kids is a map that shows you where the mine
fields are. It's a guide that tells you how your family can be
strengthened. It's a compass that teaches you how to navigate
through the hallways of schools and hospitals. It's a blueprint
that describes how you can nurture and champion your special-needs child. And most of all, it's a love letter to you, the
reader, which reveals the heart and soul of mothers and fathers
who have passed your way before.

We're living in a different day from the time when I became
paralyzed 30 years ago as a kid. Research has advanced.
Schools are more accessible. Families are more aware.
Communities are coming around. Churches are more sensitive.
Moms and dads are not so alone. I wish it had been that way
back in the 1960s. It would have made life a lot easier on my
folks. In many respects, they had no map or blueprint. But

they weren't alone. They had the best parent support group in the world, headed up by the all-time best parent ever—God Himself.

Take heart, my friend. You're not alone, either. God is on your side. And so is this book.

Joni Eareckson Tada
Disability Advocate and
President of JAF Ministries
Summer 1997

CHAPTER 1

INTRODUCTION

Cheri Fuller

A few years ago, I received a letter from Martha, a Dallas mother. She explained that she had just read my books on helping children learn and achieve, but she hadn't found exactly what she needed to help her son, Max. You see, Max suffered brain damage at birth, and his special needs were a challenge for his parents.

When her son was six years old, Martha had written Focus on the Family to get more information about what to do regarding his future and education. She had found Dr. Dobson's advice helpful. But as she told me, "In 1987 Max was just 6, but he is now 12, and 6 additional years have taken a toll on me and the entire family. Max has little time for any outside activities. We study all the time. I would just once love to talk to another Christian mom or read something another Christian mom of a slow learner or a child with disabilities has written."

She continued, "It would be so nice to hear from other Christians who can relate to what I'm going through . . . the hours I spend poring over homework with my son, the frustrations that come with the problems stemming from his brain damage, and the scriptures that help when the struggles wear you down to the breaking point." Martha had heard of similar needs from many other mothers facing various disabilities in their children, and she urged me to write a book for those parents.

God really got my attention with that mother's letter. He had already opened my eyes to the needs of parents with extraordinary kids when my niece Judy's precious daughter Natalie was born several years before. Because of a birth injury, Natalie suffered with severe cerebral palsy. I also remembered standing in the hospital waiting room with my sisters as my five-year-old niece, Evie, had open heart surgery to repair a hole in her heart. Several years later, Evie was diagnosed with juvenile rheumatoid arthritis as well.

I had personally experienced what it was like to have a chronically ill child when our firstborn son had regular, severe episodes of asthma in his early years. I had known the ache of losing a child in infancy. Our family had also felt the strain of repeated hospitalizations, daily medications, and limitations on our child, as well as recurrent anxiety about whether he would respond to medication in the emergency room and begin breathing normally again. But when Natalie was born, I was struck by the huge load on my niece in caring for her multihandicapped daughter. They lived four hours away, yet I wished I could do something to ease her load.

I had raised three children, and I had spent more than 10 years writing and speaking to parents on issues ranging from unlocking kids' learning potential to building family traditions and boosting literacy in the home. But I continued to pray that God would bring a parent of a child with special needs across my path—one who could write well and partner with me in this project. Soon after that, Louise Tucker Jones and I met at a writers' conference.

Louise Tucker Jones

Twenty years ago at the time I'm writing this, my son Jay was born with Down syndrome. Though I didn't know it at the time, God was introducing me to one of the most marvelous journeys of my life. I remember the first time I held Jay in my arms. He was wrapped cocoon fashion, from head to toe, in a white blanket. Even his face was covered. Having just been told he had Down syndrome, and knowing nothing about the disability, I was apprehensive about pulling the blanket away from his face. Would he look "different"? What would my reaction be? I had seen him only briefly in delivery before they had rushed him to a waiting isolette.

Gently, I lifted the blanket from his face. Tiny, up-slanted eyes peered out at me. His velvety forehead furrowed and wrinkled as he raised invisible blond eyebrows and opened a perfectly sculptured, little mouth. Unlike my other babies, with their full heads of dark hair, Jay's sparse, blond hair made him look bald. I unwrapped him completely to see every part of his body, counting his fingers and toes, and then wrapped him up again.

I thought back to the day when I had knelt by my bed and begged God to give me another child if it was His will, and to help me accept it if it wasn't. Our second son, Travis, had died of heart disease when he was nearly three months old, and just a year earlier, I had suffered a miscarriage. Though I had two older children, Aaron and Paula, whom I loved and adored, my heart ached for the babies I had lost. The next month, I was pregnant and ecstatic. It wasn't an easy pregnancy—early bleeding, monthly injections, an appendectomy at six months, and a breech delivery. But with each problem I could hear God whisper, "I've promised you a baby." Now here I was nine months later, a six-and-one-half-pound promise from God nestled in my arms!

Instinctively, I understood this was the moment of complete acceptance, no matter what I knew or didn't know about the future or Down syndrome. I lifted Jay's face to my own, kissed his wrinkled forehead, and vowed to him that no matter what happened, I would never, ever leave him and would love him forever. We were bonded for life. God had been faithful to give me a child. I would be faithful to accept the child He had sent.

Sometimes the way was rough—illness, heart disease, problems with school, seemingly impossible skills to learn, difficulties with communication, absence of friends, rejection, and even some problems at church. But the blessings have far outweighed the hurts. In a world where abortion quickly wipes out a life that is called "handicapped," I'm thankful that God gave me the special privilege of being the mother of one who is challenged. In so doing, He challenges me. My life is fuller. My faith is stronger. And I have more compassion for others.

Through the years, I've spoken and written about my own experiences. I've also written articles for teachers and parents of people with disabilities, started a special ministry program at my church, and often counseled parents of newborn babies with Down syndrome. When Cheri and I met and found we both had a desire to write a book for parents of children with special needs, it soon became obvious that God had brought the two of us together.

About the Book

Though we come from different perspectives and backgrounds, we share a common goal of encouraging and supporting families with children who have special needs. To do so, we set out to find the real experts—parents who are raising or have raised a medically fragile or disabled child—and ask what their challenges were and how they coped in everyday life. We discovered that most parents—whatever their child's disability or medical condition—face common problems and struggle with the same questions:

- How can I deal with the diagnosis, with grief, and with other feelings and come to acceptance of my child's condition?

- How can I deal with medical professionals, therapists, and the reams of technical medical information to get the best care for my child?

- How can I become an effective advocate for my child's needs in educational issues and in the classroom without being intimidated?

- How can we find the support and services we need as a family?

- How can we strengthen our marriage, since approximately 85 percent of the marriages of couples with a special-needs child end in divorce? How can we find time to be together and communicate effectively?

- How can the church better minister to special children and their families?

We also began to look at ways to deal with extended family and grandparents, promote healthy sibling relationships, and handle your own anxiety in the medical crises you may face. We explored how to pray for your child, for your own needs, and for many other areas. Parents were looking for ideas and practical solutions. We tried to tackle these and other common issues with God's grace, with a biblical perspective on families and children, and most of all with our strong belief in the worth of every individual.

We don't have all the answers, but we've talked with dozens of parents who have kept their families and faith intact and have learned invaluable lessons that God taught them. We learned so much by hearing their stories! Some of the stories will tug at your heart. Some will make you laugh. But they will all give you hope and encouragement—something for which every parent of a child with a special challenge or problem is looking.

This book is for many kinds of people:

- Parents of a child with any kind of disability, chronic or acute illness, or who is medically fragile

- Grandparents and extended family of a child with special needs

- Therapists and physicians

- Public- and private-school teachers

- Sunday school teachers and pastors, since we

all need to find ways to relate to, minister to,
and embrace those with disabilities and allow
them to be a real, functioning part of both our
communities and the Body of Christ.

More than 90 percent of the primary caregivers for children
with special needs are their mothers, so this book was written
with them primarily in mind. But we know lots of dads are
involved, too, so we've also included anecdotes and tips that
will help them as fathers.

In John chapter 9, when Jesus healed the man who was born
blind, His disciples quizzed Him about whose fault this blind-
ness was: "Rabbi, who sinned, this man or his parents, that he
was born blind?" (verse 2).

"Neither this man nor his parents sinned," Jesus answered
them (verse 3). He went on to say this happened so that the
work of God—the glory of God—might be displayed in the
man's life.

That's what we've heard, seen, and experienced as we have
interviewed parents, listened to their stories, and written this
book: the glory of God displayed in the lives of these families
and a clearer view of His love. For example, consider the following account that Karen Wingate, a Kansas mother, told us
about her baby daughter's first surgery:

When the surgical nurse took my baby out of my
arms, I shuddered. I couldn't let her go. I had hardly
had time to bond with her. My milk began to drip
down my front as my whole body yearned for my
baby. "Oh, God," I cried inwardly, "after nine surgeries
on my own eyes, I hate surgery. But I would go in
there myself if it would give her perfect vision!" Tears

streamed down my face as my husband led me to the elevator. Then it struck me. That's what Jesus did. He went into the "operating room" Himself, to mend the deficit of sin, so that our souls would be perfect before God. The kind of love and yearning I experience for my daughter was a small glimpse of the great love God has for His children and of His longing for them.

In the midst of the struggles, heartaches, and sometimes almost overwhelming difficulties of parenting a child with special needs, God's grace has been evident, His faithfulness shown time and again. It's our hope and prayer that this book might be a window for you, too, to see His grace and glory a little more clearly.

For those of you who are parenting a child with special needs and facing whatever problems—either everyday ones or perhaps a major surgery on the horizon—we pray that in these pages you will find comfort, encouragement, some laughter, and practical resources for the many challenges you might face now or in the years ahead. And we pray that by reading the stories of parents who walk a similar path, you will most of all find *hope.*

Praise be to the God and Father of our Lord Jesus Christ, the Father of compassion and the God of all comfort, who comforts us in all our troubles, so that we can comfort those in any trouble with the comfort we ourselves have received from God.
(2 Corinthians 1:3-4)

DEALING WITH DIAGNOSIS AND MOVING TOWARD ACCEPTANCE

"What's wrong with my baby?" Marilyn Phillips asked her pediatrician. "She screams and is constantly sick. Nothing helps." Marilyn and her husband, Nolen, prayed that doctors would discover the cause of their daughter's problems. They felt hopeless.

At three months old, Rebekah was hospitalized for a battery of tests. While waiting for the results, Marilyn fired angry questions at God: "Why is my baby so sick? What's wrong with her?" Then she demanded, "We must have some answers!"

When the tests were completed, a young intern came into

Welcome to ...
Holland!
by Emily Pearl Kingsley

I am often asked to describe the experience of raising a child with a disability—to try to help people who have not shared that unique experience to understand it, to imagine how it would feel. It's like this ...

When you're going to have a baby, it's like planning a fabulous vacation trip—to Italy. You buy a bunch of guidebooks and make your wonderful plans. The Coliseum. The Michelangelo David. The gondolas in Venice. You may learn some handy phrases in Italian. It's all very exciting.

After months of eager anticipation, the day finally arrives. You pack your bags, and off you go. Several hours later, the plane lands. The flight attendant comes and says, "Welcome to Holland."

"Holland?!" you say. "What do you mean, Holland? I signed up for Italy! I'm supposed to be in Italy. All my life I've dreamed of going to Italy."

But there's been a change in the flight plan. They've landed in

the room and said, "One test is positive. Your daughter has cystic fibrosis, or CF for short." Talking in a monotone, the intern proceeded with frightening information concerning CF: It's inherited; it's the most common fatal genetic disease; it's incurable. Pausing for a moment, he added, "An average life expectancy for a CF patient is only 13 years. However, don't start building up your hopes, because many children don't live even that long. Chances are that your child will die a CF-related death at a very early age." Glancing at Rebekah, the doctor left the room. All hope for their daughter's future had vanished.

Incurable! How that word tore at Marilyn's aching heart! She had read articles dealing with people afflicted by incurable diseases, but she had never known anyone with such an illness. In fact, her immediate family had never even experienced the death of a loved one; all her grandparents were still healthy and living full lives.

Devastated, Marilyn couldn't

even say "CF" without breaking into tears. She wondered if their daughter would be the first family member to die. Being Christians, she and her husband turned immediately to God. *Maybe if we pray, He will miraculously heal her, and then others will come to know Him through this,* she thought.

"You think that if you pray hard enough or have more faith, your child will be healed," she says now. "We even had close friends who challenged us that if we had more faith she would be healed, and then the guilt came: Is it our fault?"

Over time, Nolen and Marilyn realized God's answer was that their daughter *did* have CF, *He would be with them,* and they needed to go on from there. Once they could accept this, the Phillipses started to see God's hand in their lives. They also were excited when Rebekah's first therapist accepted Jesus as her Savior after seeing how Rebekah's family handled CF, realizing something was missing in her own life.

Holland, and there you must stay.

The important thing is that they haven't taken you to a horrible, disgusting, filthy place full of pestilence, famine, and disease. It's just a different place.

So you must go out and buy new guidebooks. And you must learn a whole new language. And you will meet a whole new group of people you otherwise would never have met.

It's just a different place. It's slower paced than Italy, less flashy than Italy. But after you've been there for a while, you catch your breath, look around, and begin to notice that Holland has windmills, tulips, and even Rembrandts.

But everyone you know is busy coming and going from Italy, and they're all bragging about what a wonderful time they had there. And for the rest of your life you will say, "Yes, that's where I was supposed to go. That's what I had planned."

And the pain of that will never, ever go away, because the loss of that dream is a significant loss.

But if you spend your life mourning the fact that you didn't get to Italy, you may never be free to enjoy the very special and very lovely things about Holland.

The Phillipses didn't have any promises about Rebekah's life span, but they did have God's promises in the Bible. The one that meant the most was Psalm 139:16, which says, "All the days ordained for me were written in your book before one of them came to be." Embracing the truth that God knows the beginning from the end and had planned each day of their daughter's life, they began to celebrate each day and focus on the positive.

Acceptance didn't mean Marilyn escaped the grieving process, however. "You assume your daughter will wear your wedding dress," she says, "and I experienced grief because it might never happen. It's like a death of visions for the future, and it doesn't just happen one time." But some of her dreams have actually come true. At six years old, Rebekah danced in a pink tutu; in high school she was a cheerleader; now she's a freshman in college. And with all the advances in treatment, some CF patients are living into their twenties.

Delayed Diagnosis

From the beginning, Julie Shanafelt knew something was wrong with her son, Jason, but she didn't have a diagnosis. Finally, after many tests and countless doctors' appointments, at five years old he was diagnosed with fragile X, a chromosome disorder.

Until then, Julie had clung to the idea that he was just a little delayed and would eventually catch up. But with the diagnosis, she finally had to realize Jason was not going to catch up miraculously to his peers.

With dreams shattered, anger enveloped Julie. "My anger was not so much toward God but selfishly at all the things I was going to have to give up, like my husband and I living out our retirement alone," she says. "Guilt also set in because fragile X is hereditary, and we discovered I was the carrier. Nobody made me feel guilty. I put it all on myself."

But the greatest problem Julie faced was fear: "I feared my inadequacies and my inability to live up to the challenges that lay ahead. I feared the future. For the next three years, I lived with these feelings, stuffing them deep down inside. I trudged on, doing the best I could with Jason, but never with joy and acceptance because I was clinging to anger, guilt, and fear."

After attending a conference held by Joni Eareckson Tada and reading a number of Joni's books, Julie came across a concept that changed her life. "In the world's eyes, Jason is not perfect," Julie says, "but God sees him as perfect and complete because he has God's perfect Holy Spirit." God used this same concept to teach her who she is in Christ—and that she, too, has handicaps, though they're not visible.

"For the first time in 30 years, I saw myself perfect and complete in Christ," she continues. "I can't even express what this concept has done for me. It was at that point that I fell on my knees and humbly thanked God for bringing Jason into my life and for using him to teach me. All the anger, guilt, and fear immediately left at that point. What once was a drudgery is now a joy. What once was a frustration is now a blessing. Through Jason, I was given a visual picture of God's attributes—unconditional love, mercy, peace, encouragement, help, and comfort."

Express Your Feelings

Whether receiving a diagnosis at birth or several years later, like Julie, many parents of children with special needs are completely overwhelmed when told their children have a disability or serious illness. Their world has been shaken. Dreams have been shattered. Hope may even seem far away. They may be catapulted into an immediate medical crisis. There are so many unknowns. They may be struggling with feelings of anger, guilt, denial, or fear.

Don't deny those feelings in your own heart. Be still. Rest. Cry if you need to. Allow yourself to grieve. Also, remember that parents often grieve differently. Dads may have a harder time expressing their emotions than moms, but they still need the same support. Take the advice of some parents who have traveled the road you are on:

- "Be kind to yourself!" says Sarah Aldridge. "Give yourself time to adjust. Let the other spouse have the freedom to *not* be where you are emotionally until he or she is ready. Pamper yourself when stress hits. Don't expect too much of yourself. Grieving will turn into acceptance, but it takes time."

- "Pray for yourself and for wisdom to lead your child in the right path and not block God's plan for your child," suggests Paula Sisler. "Also, try not to be overprotective."

- "Don't feel you have to explain everything to everyone you meet," says Valerie Stewart.

- Cindy Richards advises, "Don't look too far forward or too far backward. Concentrate on *today*."

- "Be honest with your feelings," says Virginia Reddick. "Don't feel guilty when you feel frustrated or want to give up. It won't always be easy or feel like a blessing, but God will honor your endurance and give you the strength to handle every situation."

- This advice came from a social worker to the parents of a child with CF: "Your attitude about CF and whether you accept it will affect your child's life and whether she will be able to accept it." (This could be said of most disabilities.)

- Louise Stewart tells of a letter she received from her uncle soon after her son was born. "You have lost an expectation, but you have gained a child," he said. She continues, "How true that was. Pregnancy is about having a child. Our dreams and expectations for our child may not always become a reality, but we still have that new life we desperately wanted to begin with." And this advice came from her pediatrician: *This is your child. Love him!*

- Gayla Syed says, "Emma is my balance in life. She makes me look at things in a simple light."

- Pam Whitley reminds parents that God is always the final authority: "Lay any negative diagnosis at His feet, and listen for His direction. It makes all the difference in the world."

- A doctor shared this wisdom with me (Louise): "Don't let anyone put a number on Jay's days!"

I hope you also will take that message to heart.
Don't let fear of a disability, an illness, or the
future rule your life. God is sovereign!

Double Diagnosis

Helen Mitchell's daughter, Megan, was misdiagnosed with
cerebral palsy (CP) at eight months of age. "I had a hard time
with Megan's diagnosis, wondering what I did wrong," Helen
says. "We were fixing up a house to move into while I was
pregnant, so I wondered if I had lifted something heavy or
smelled too many fumes while painting."

Then Helen switched gears, thinking that if she worked hard
enough with Megan's therapy, everything would be okay in
three or four years.

When her son, Mitch, was born nearly four years later,
Helen watched his progress carefully. Though he progressed in
some ways that Megan didn't, Mitch was diagnosed with spastic quadriplegia, a genetic disorder, at four months.

On the surface, the problem appeared to be severe CP, but
with both children being unable to use their limbs or to speak,
the doctors searched for a better diagnosis. Megan's diagnosis
was also changed to spastic quadriplegia. Neither child will
ever be independent, and both are in wheelchairs.

Helen again felt guilty after Mitch was diagnosed, since it
was a genetic condition. For a while, she didn't even want to
leave the house. It was a hard time, with a lot of grief to work
through.

Gradually, however, Helen developed a positive attitude.
Both children are very bright and use eye blinks for *yes* or *no*.
At 16 and 12, they both model for the J. C. Penney catalog.
The makeup artists tease Megan about her boyfriend until the

cameraman gets that perfect smile. When a new catalog comes out, Megan takes it to school in her book bag. "It helps her to interact with other students," says her mom. And last year, the high school newspaper did a special article on Megan and her modeling.

Replacing Dreams

Sometimes broken dreams can be replaced with a new reality. Since Helen loved to sew, she dreamed about all the things she was going to make for her daughter someday. "I could picture myself making a rag doll with a cheerleading uniform to match Megan's when she got to be a teenager," she says. Although that didn't happen, her sewing has still been beneficial. She can take patterns and adjust them to fit Megan properly, which is especially valuable since her daughter is in a wheelchair. And she still makes a doll for Megan's stocking every Christmas.

When Helen finds herself with a case of the blues, she pulls out a J. C. Penney catalog and sees two *model* children who belong to her. That always brings a smile!

Why, God?

After Tammy Townsend's daughter, Brittany, was diagnosed with Rett syndrome, Tammy's faith took a beating. She explains: "I kept saying to God, 'I can't read Your stories or parables in the Bible. I can't sit here and try to apply something from somebody else's life to my life. How am I supposed to handle this? What's in the future? What's going on? I've got to talk to You! I know You're trying to talk with me, but I just can't hear it. You're going to have to get in my face and tell me how I'm supposed to deal with this. I have so many questions for You.'"

One day at a women's retreat, God revealed Himself to Tammy. "Kay Arthur was speaking on the death of Jesus," she says, "and I just kept crying and saying, 'I just didn't know You had to go through all that.' My heart was right to accept things from Jesus at that time. When I closed my eyes to pray, I saw a bright light. I opened them, thinking it was something in the auditorium, but it wasn't. I closed them again and realized it was the presence of Jesus, and I thought, *Oh, I've got so much to ask You,* but I couldn't ask anything. It wasn't even important anymore. I was so overwhelmed by His presence—the all-encompassing holiness—that I could then see how you could go to heaven and spend eternity just praising Him. There was such greatness! And in that moment, God showed me that 'Why?' was not important, but *He* was what was important.

"'Why?' is not going to explain the world to me. But I do understand some things a little better. I see that our lifestyle is good for Brittany. We go a lot of places and do lots of outdoor things together that are very good for her. I believe God thought a lot about what we needed and what Brittany needed and then put the three of us together."

Self-pity has also been thrown out the window. "I gave in one time soon after Brittany was diagnosed," Tammy says. "I sat on the floor and sobbed into a pillow, 'I can't handle it!' Suddenly, Brittany came barreling across the room, giggling, and I thought, *Who am I feeling sorry for? It's certainly not her, because she's perfectly content with the way she is.* That ended my self-pity."

Nor does Tammy pray for Brittany to be healed anymore. "I don't want her different!" Tammy says. "When I thought I had a normal child and found out she was handicapped, I felt like I lost my other child. Now I don't want to lose the child I have."

And one of Tammy's greatest rewards from being a mom of a

child with special needs is that she has a deeper relationship with Jesus Christ. "I wouldn't trade that for anything!" she concludes. "Sometimes I think He chose me to be a mom just for that reason."

Daddy Stays Home

When Eric and Melanie Stevens's first child, Hunter, was born with severe medical problems, there was no question about who would stay home with him. Melanie had the insurance, working for Blue Cross and Blue Shield. And since their children's medical bills have now exceeded $600,000, they're glad they made the choice for Eric to become "Mr. Mom." Four-year-old Hunter is the picture of perfect health now, but he didn't start out that way. At one week old, he suffered congestive heart failure, followed by brain surgery at four months, then another heart problem.

Two years later, their daughter, Ashley, was born with only three out of eight sections of her brain functioning, the result of a stroke in utero. "She can hear and her organs work," says her dad, "but her digestive system doesn't work properly.

"It was really tough," Eric continues, "but easier than what I went through with Hunter, because I wasn't a Christian then." And Ashley does so much more than the doctors ever gave them hope of seeing. "She shouldn't be able to recognize us, but she does. Her brain is nothing but fluid, yet she smiles, laughs, kicks, and gives us kisses. She's a miracle!"

But being a Christian didn't take away the grief of having a chronically ill child. Eric and Melanie struggled with "Why?" along with disbelief and anger, but like other parents they worked their way through grief into acceptance. "You can feel sorry for yourself and blame God," Eric says, "or you can do something to help other people. Second Corinthians 1:3-4 says, 'Praise be to the God and Father of our Lord Jesus Christ, the Father of compassion and the God of all comfort, who comforts us in all our troubles, so that we can comfort those in any trouble with the comfort we ourselves have received from God.' God *has* comforted us, so we feel the need to comfort others."

Eric and Melanie have opened their home to other parents who have chronically ill children in the hospital. "They know that we know what they're going through," says Eric. "Our desire is that when people see Ashley, they see God. When people who stay in our home question us, we tell them we're only able to do what we do because of Christ."

One of God's Miracles

One of the hardest times for the Stevenses was when Ashley was a year old. She cried nonstop, screaming in pain, for up to 20 hours a day in spite of being on heavy sedatives. Another surgery, one of many, was performed to put a feeding line into her intestine rather than her stomach in hopes of minimizing the problem. But the pain and screaming continued. The doctor said she would always live in pain equivalent to that of a woman in labor multiplied by seven.

Melanie and Eric had prayed for Ashley all her life—that she would hold her head up, have partial sight, laugh aloud, and so on. But when Ashley's pain became nonstop, they released her to God. "Before, we asked for small miracles," says Eric. "Now we asked God to either heal her and leave her with us or take her home and heal her. We didn't want her suffering like that."

And God answered their prayer. "He gave us a miracle," Eric

says. "Ashley isn't in pain anymore. She is one happy little girl!"

The Stevenses, in turn, are one happy family that wouldn't trade places with anyone. "After this experience, I finally look at God as 'Daddy,'" says Eric. "When I hurt, I can go to my heavenly Father, crawl up in His lap, and let Him love me just the way Hunter does with me. God gives us so much grace. His grace is number one!"

These devoted parents have not given up hope for a complete recovery for Ashley, either. "When you give up hope, you give up on her," Tammy says. "Realistically, I know she shouldn't do anything, but God has the final say."

Working Through Grief

As a nurse and parent of a son with Down syndrome, Joanne Woolsey is often called on to counsel parents of newborn Down babies. She tells them how much families come to love children with Down syndrome—it seems to be universal. But she also tells them it's okay to grieve. "You have to grieve for the child you were expecting before you can accept the child you have," she says.

Some stages of grief that you might experience are:

- *Denial.* I can't believe this is happening to me.

- *Anxiety.* How can I possibly handle this?

- *Fear.* What will happen to my child and my family?

- *Guilt.* What did I do to cause this?

- *Depression.* My hopes and dreams seem to be lost forever.

- *Anger.* This isn't fair!

- *Acceptance.* I don't like what has happened. I don't understand *why* it happened. I don't know how I'm going to handle this. But God knows, and I can trust Him.

You may go through the above stages several times. You may get stuck in one stage or get to acceptance and then go back to anger, fear, or more grieving when a different situation or milestone comes into your life. It may be a long, ongoing process or a short, one-time process. Grief tailor-makes itself according to what each individual is going through. For some parents, the grief *never* stops; it just pauses now and then. One of the keys to surviving grief is to allow yourself to experience it. Recognize it and receive God's comfort.

Grief Comes Unexpectedly

Sandy Rios tells how grief can be ongoing with a multihandicapped or total-care child: "Something hits you and you revisit grief with all its intensity." Once she was sitting in church with her daughter, Sasha, who was eight or nine at the time but still could not sit up, and a children's choir came in to sing. The grief Sandy felt was like a knife in her heart, and her feelings of loss were intense.

The same thing happened at a 20-year college reunion, when Sandy met old friends and everyone started pulling out pictures of their children. Like Sandy, five of her friends had daughters, two of them beauty queens. "I mourned the whole weekend," says Sandy. She was thrilled for her friends, but she realized anew what she had lost. Finally, on Sasha's sixteenth birthday, Sandy recognized that she was spending so much time mourning her loss that she had failed to celebrate who Sasha was. At that point, Sandy began to really heal.

During an especially difficult time, only the Holy Spirit can interpret our pain to the Father. Romans 8:26 says, "The Spirit himself intercedes for us with groans that words cannot express." Sandy found that if she cried out to God in agony, it brought relief. "When you're filled with that much grief, embrace it or you don't heal," she says. "It will play itself out later as resentment, bitterness, lack of faith, or hardness toward God and other people. But if we express our feelings, God comes and comforts us."

Looking for Joy

Stephanie Alexander felt guilty when her daughter, Audrey, was born with spina bifida. "I thought I was being punished because I had quit going to church," Stephanie says. Her husband, Carl, had never stopped going to church, so she put the full blame on herself. "Every time we would face some new problem, I'd start crying and say, 'I know God is punishing me.' Finally Carl said, 'I'm really tired of hearing you say that. She is not punishment! How can you look at her and think she's punishment to you?'"

Stephanie realized her husband was right. She turned back to God and also sought help from another mom of a child with spina bifida. "We talked a long time," Stephanie says. "That was the beginning of my healing." Now Stephanie feels grateful for everything Audrey does. "When my son, Gregg, walked, I was happy, but when Audrey walked, the joy was deep in my soul. It's so great to see her overcome anything—I celebrate life so much differently."

Divine Wisdom

Even with the best of doctors, support groups, friends, and family, parents don't always find the answers to those questions and thoughts that play over and over in their minds. There are no easy answers. Time, prayer, and experience help, but nothing replaces divine guidance from Scripture. Through His Word, God places a healing balm on our hearts and emotions. If you're struggling with any of the questions below, perhaps these thoughts and scriptures will help:

- *What did I do wrong in pregnancy?* Don't drive yourself crazy with this thought. You probably did all the right things—good prenatal care, regular checkups, and so on.

  "Before I formed you in the womb I knew you" (Jeremiah 1:5).

- *How can I find the strength to handle this?* You can take one day at a time. Do what has to be done, and when you don't know what else to do, just do the next thing.

  "My grace is sufficient for you, for my power is made perfect in weakness" (2 Corinthians 12:9).

- *Will this child live with me forever?* Probably not, but none of us has any guarantees. There are many alternatives for adults with special needs (see chapter 13), and most *want* to be independent. Some of these adults choose to live at home because they have a job, friends, church, and parents who enjoy them and don't want them to leave.

"Whoever welcomes one of these little children in my name welcomes me" (Mark 9:37).

• *What if I don't feel blessed or joyful the way some parents talk about?* Give yourself time to adjust. Joy and blessings may not be visible right away. They come softly and quietly, when you least expect them.

"The LORD is close to the brokenhearted and saves those who are crushed in spirit" (Psalm 34:18).

• *Will our lives ever be normal again?* There's no definition of *normal*. What's normal for you may be foreign to others. Choose your own normalcy.

"I have come that they may have life, and have it to the full" (John 10:10).

• *What if my child dies?* The death of any child is more than a parent can bear outside of Jesus Christ as your comforter. Fix your thoughts on Him.

"I will never leave you nor forsake you" (Joshua 1:5).

Allow yourself time to adjust to whatever circumstances you face. Don't try to handle a lifetime of problems in one day. See your child through the eyes of God; let His Word filter your vision.

Steps to Acceptance

Martha Little, mother of a child with special needs, offers the following steps to acceptance:

- *Acknowledge* that God's hand was on your child or children in the way they were formed before birth, according to His plan.

- *Admit* any areas you resent in the way God made them.

- *Accept* God's design for them. Thank Him for their personalities and the way they are.

- *Affirm* God's purpose in creating them for His glory.

- *Ally* yourself with God in His plans for them.

"Our job is to see our children as God does and to involve ourselves in His plans, not our own," Martha says.

The Gift of Children

When Jay was diagnosed with heart disease, I (Louise) asked God, "Why?" When Jay couldn't communicate, I asked, "Why?" When he tried to be like other children and was rejected, I asked, "Why, God?" But those challenges never fazed Jay. He just kept right on celebrating life.

Then one day I read an article about a businessman who was blind. He explained that he was often introduced as "handicapped," so he decided to investigate the word. He stated, "The dictionary says a handicap is an added burden given to a superior contender to equalize the contest." I caught my breath at that definition and thought, *That's Jay! He often experiences rejection, yet he returns acceptance. He's stared at, taunted, teased, and sees prejudice in its ugliest form, yet he forgives with a hug and a kiss.*

Jay has proved to be a superior contender in life, and he has taught me so much about love. Today when I ask why, I ask with a totally different perspective. I ask, "Why, God? Why am I so blessed with this beautiful, sensitive child? How could You entrust me with this tender creation?"

I have no idea why God allowed me to be Jay's mom, but I'm so glad He did. I can't tell you why God allowed the things that are happening in your life, but God will use them to His glory. Somehow we need to understand that He loves us with a love greater than anything we can possibly comprehend and wants to teach us how to celebrate life in the midst of challenges. He made and gave us every one of our children, and He knew everything about them before they were ever born. They are gifts—precious gifts from God—and He makes no mistakes!

Encouragement from Scripture

- "Be joyful always; pray continually; give thanks in all circumstances, for this is God's will for you in Christ Jesus" (1 Thessalonians 5:16-18).

- "Let us then approach the throne of grace with confidence, so that we may receive mercy and find grace to help us in our time of need" (Hebrews 4:16).

- "He has made everything beautiful in its time" (Ecclesiastes 3:11).

- "You have seen me tossing and turning through the night. You have collected all my tears and preserved them in your bottle! You have recorded every one in your book" (Psalm 56:8, TLB).

- "And my God will meet all your needs according to his glorious riches in Christ Jesus" (Philippians 4:19).

- "Even when we are too weak to have any faith left, he remains faithful to us and will help us" (2 Timothy 2:13, TLB).

- "So take a new grip with your tired hands, stand firm on your shaky legs, and mark out a straight, smooth path for your feet so that those who follow you, though weak and lame, will not fall and hurt themselves, but become strong" (Hebrews 12:12-13, TLB).

- "Children are a gift from God" (Psalm 127:3, TLB).

CHAPTER 3

FINDING A NETWORK OF SUPPORT

Parents cope better with the challenges of raising a child with special needs or disabilities when they have regular interaction with other parents in the same situation. Such support helps to strengthen them, and it's also the source of some of the best information on how to cope with their child's needs, solve problems, and find the best physicians, therapists, and equipment.

After securing the best possible medical care for your child, your next main focus needs to be finding a support system. It may be that your family (if they live close by and can offer help), your church, or your prayer group are already supporting you. But meeting regularly with parents who have children with medical needs similar to your child's or joining a group of moms and dads whose children have a variety of disabilities is still one of the most worthwhile things you can do.

As Louise Stewart says, "I came to realize over the past few years that no matter what the handicap, parents generally endure many similar difficulties medically and emotionally. They've been where you are or are going through the same thing you're going through now. They know how you feel and what you're experiencing internally." When you can share with another parent the emotional experience of being up all night five nights in a row, or of how scared you were about a negative report from the doctor, you realize you aren't the only one who has gone through this experience. You also find solutions to certain problems.

But perhaps one of the best reasons to attend a parent support group is that having a special-needs child can be an isolating experience. "When you first have a handicapped child, you're on center stage and everybody's there," said one physician. He explained that your friends and family are in the front row—you may have 30 people supporting you in the hospital waiting room.

In the first weeks, they bring you food every day, and you're thankful. But as every month goes by, they move back one row and then another, and soon they're in the rear of the auditorium. Their lives are going on; they've pulled back to their everyday interests and seem assured that you've gotten your life together as well. Thus, the help offered decreases greatly. They think it's normal to see you in the situation, yet you're still right where you were, in a survival mode, particularly if your child requires total care. You have the same or even more responsibilities a few months or years down the road, but you have less support.

We hope family members, friends, and fellow church members are going to be supportive. But with this new and challenging dimension of your life, you may well need a parent support group. With them, since they have similar needs and interests, you don't have to explain every little detail and can quickly get to your major subjects of concern. These new friends will share a bond with you and add to your already existing network of friends.

Getting together in parent support groups can take a variety of forms, as the different types of groups that follow show. Some groups' meetings feature discussions, films, and speakers. Others are not as structured. Most offer a place to talk, share experiences, and laugh again. "We've frequently caught ourselves laughing at situations about our children that people who are not living the nightmare would never understand and definitely not find amusing," said one mother. "Laughing at difficult situations with people who understand makes us feel human again! And when you start to turn your resentment and self-pity to helping others who are also hurting, your pain somehow seems to lessen."

Motivation, Courage, and Friendship

Sometimes the information gained at just one meeting can be critically important. The summer Dottie Jones was trying to decide whether to mainstream her profoundly deaf son, Chris, in the neighborhood middle school, she attended a parent support meeting. There the speaker, a college girl who was also profoundly deaf, described her experiences of being mainstreamed in a regular junior high and high school. Dottie realized her son had many of the same personality traits that had helped this girl cope. And Dottie was struck by the benefits this girl communicated and how her mainstreaming experience had equipped her to succeed in college.

"Hearing this young speaker gave me the boost, courage, and extra motivation I needed to ask the school district for what we felt was best for Chris," Dottie says. "I don't think I would have had the assertiveness without hearing her firsthand experience."

Another benefit is the relationship between parents. When the infant stimulation teacher came into the Meines' home to work with Natalie each week, she realized Judy (the mom) knew none of the parents all over the Carrollton, Texas, community whom she served in early childhood intervention programs. So the teacher started a parent support group. The children from these families had different disabilities, but the parents had a common bond.

"I got to know other mothers and enjoy some new friend-ships," Judy says. "At that point, many of my other friends who didn't have a disabled child couldn't relate to what we were going through with Natalie." One evening they had a potluck supper and a speaker. Other nights there were social opportunities that included their children, because sometimes it was hard to find child care in the evenings. Fathers who came benefited from talking to other dads. These parents learned about special pro-grams, equipment, and services that they otherwise wouldn't have known about. And ten years later, some of those parents are still friends.

Grandparents and extended family members can also benefit from participating in a support group. It helps them understand more of what the parents are going through and how to help them. And in the process, the grandparents can also find accep-tance for the disabled child. Sometimes a parent's most difficult obstacle is educating family members so they can and will pro-vide support. Attending a support group of families with special needs can provide grandparents with plenty of ideas on how to relate to their grandchildren and offer help to the family.

In addition, there are support groups for siblings of children with disabilities or chronic illness. In those meetings, kids can meet other siblings in a relaxed, recreational setting to discuss the special challenges, concerns, and joys they experience, gain information, and learn how to handle common situations. Problems that other kids don't face—like defending a sibling from name-calling, responding to questions from friends, and coping with high expectations or a lack of attention from parents—are just a few of the concerns addressed in a sibling support group. Check the resource section at the back of this book for sibling assistance programs.

Connecting with Other Parents: National and Regional Support Organizations

You can find significant support from national organizations. Connecting with another family and attending a Williams syndrome regional parent meeting helped Valerie and Dale Campbell come out of denial and face up to their son's condition. When Brian was diagnosed, there was no definitive test, so physicians based the diagnosis on his heart problem, facial features (small, upturned nose, curly hair, full lips and cheeks, and small teeth), and behavior—things you can't measure with a test. Williams syndrome is a rare (1 out of every 20,000 births) neurobehavioral congenital disorder. It affects several areas of development, including cognitive, behavioral (attention difficulties), and motor areas. Many children with Williams syndrome have mental retardation.

Since the Campbells didn't see anything unusual about Brian's features and thought anybody could have a heart problem, it was hard for them to accept the diagnosis. They didn't even tell anyone for several years that he had Williams syndrome, because they were in denial. They felt that if they didn't accept it, maybe it wouldn't be true.

Then one day Dale read a newspaper article about a child in Houston with Williams syndrome, and he got the family's phone number through the paper. Since he and Valerie had been told there were only about 100 cases in the U.S. and they had never met anyone with Williams syndrome, parenting Brian had been a lonely experience. But through hearing this family's stories and the similarities between their children, Valerie and Dale began to move toward acceptance.

"Also, I was encouraged because the mother sounded so positive," says Valerie. "I was feeling so much despair, and she made me feel like it wasn't the end of the world." From this mom, she also found out about the Williams Syndrome Association.

Months later, when the Campbells attended a conference with other parents and children with Williams syndrome, a real awakening occurred. "All these children looked like Brian did at that age—they all had this friendly personality, had similar facial features, and could have been brothers and sisters!" Valerie says. "I shed a lot of tears, and it was hard, but it was a big step in helping us overcome the denial. I don't think you can be as effective in helping your child until you move out of denial to acceptance. Otherwise you think, *He's going to be normal someday—he just needs more therapy or infant stimulation.* We were freed to focus on: What does this child really need, and how can we help him?"

That's what they began to discover at the Williams syndrome conference: how best to help their son. They felt comfortable asking other parents, "Do you have this kind of problem with your child, and how do you deal with it?" For example, Brian didn't have the coordination to ride a bicycle, which they found frustrating. One of the other parents suggested they buy him a low-riding Big Wheel—and he loved it! In addition, the Campbells were able to confer with cardiologists there about Brian's upcoming heart surgery.

They found the parent meetings a nonthreatening environment, and their participation in them became part of the healing process. They trusted the information they got from other parents of Williams syndrome children because they had experience. "We actually got more information from parents than from the medical people—it wasn't as clinical but was more practical and useful for our daily life with Brian," says Dale.

In the beginning, the support organization helped the Campbells to cope with their child. But as they got comfortable in the group and with addressing their problems, the value changed; they began to look for ways to give back to others. "We've come from just receiving to experiencing our greatest benefit: seeing the satisfaction of helping parents who are struggling just as we were," says Dale. That's why they now serve as regional directors of the Williams Syndrome Association. They found that when they share what they've learned, they can be a lifeline to another family.

Up-to-Date Research and Information

In addition to providing support, national organizations can link you to vital information. From the beginning of their daughter's diagnosis, Marilyn and Nolen Phillips were put in contact with the Cystic Fibrosis Foundation, from which they gained a wealth of knowledge. They were given research information even before it appeared in the newspaper, as well as brochures to give to their daughter's teachers describing what to expect and how to help her in the classroom.

"We're very informed about what's going on in genetics, and the foundation updates us continually about new information," says Marilyn. They found out about new, aggressive treatments that improved Rebekah's health, and an enzyme developed recently has made a tremendous difference in what she can eat and digest.

Nelda Cimmerman, a Dallas mother, was involved recently with an international parent-to-parent support-group conference that drew more than 2,000 parents of children with disabilities from all over the world. Whether it's a small support group or a large one, she finds these gatherings "help you know you're not alone and you're not crazy! Many times, other parents share with us solutions they've found for common problems, and other parents give us creative ideas of how they take care of themselves and their marriages."

In the resource section at the back of this book, you'll find a list of national organizations for many specific disabilities, along with information about how to contact them.

Help in Time of Need

James and Kathy were parents of a 21-year-old son with developmental disabilities. Kathy had cancer, and often, without warning and in the middle of the night, she had to be taken to the hospital for blood transfusions. In a support group meeting, James voiced his concern about leaving their son home alone: "I worry about Kathy, but also about our son. What if I couldn't get back home for a long while? I'm not sure he could manage."

By the time the meeting was over, James and Kathy had a list of names and phone numbers of caring friends willing to help them day *or* night.

Sometimes a support group allows younger parents to glean strength and encouragement from parents of an older handicapped person. Diane and Mark are parents of a one-year-old mentally handicapped son. Sue is a single parent of a 40-year-old handicapped son. A strong and trusting relationship has developed between Diane, Mark, and Sue. The young couple often seeks Sue's advice and encouragement.

One night when their group meeting was almost over, the leader asked if anyone had questions or special concerns. After hesitating a few moments, Diane asked Sue, "When does the crying stop?"

Sue stood, went over to Diane, gave her a big hug, and said, "Never . . . but it will be all right." She went on to assure Diane that, as with any child, the joys and laughter would outweigh the sorrow. Here again was a true, experienced friend—listening, lifting, and loving.

Single Parenting a Special-Needs Child

The single parent has unique needs and stresses, especially if he or she is the sole caretaker of a disabled child. One of the biggest pitfalls is the tendency to neglect your own needs. As Rosemarie Cook says, "We parents of children with special needs often forget how to take care of ourselves. We may be able to get along fine until some major stress or crisis develops. If we continue to ignore our own needs, we will suffer the consequences, mentally or physically or both. . . . It's a natural reaction to want to compensate for the loss in our children's lives, whether that loss is by death or divorce." She suggests several ways to cope and keep balance in your life as a single parent:

Find a network of support, whether that's in a kinship or fellowship group at your church, a disability support group, or one of the many other kinds available. When the usual support of a spouse is missing, it's easy to focus even more on your child's needs and put greater stress on yourself. You may have to rebuild a system of support, which could include a combination of family, friends, church, and a monthly or weekly group so you aren't bearing all the burdens alone. Having others with whom you can discuss options and decisions on things like schooling and medical care is helpful. And making time to go to lunch or a movie with a friend can provide needed communication and recreation.

Work through anger to forgiveness, and deal with unresolved problems. This will help you be healthier emotionally, spiritually, and physically, and thus a better parent.

Whenever possible, keep both parents involved in your child's life, and share in the decision-making process.

Learn to rely on God. This is one of the best ways to deal with the many challenges of raising a disabled child single-handedly. "I would be the last person to say I have the answers to life as a single custodial parent," says Rosemarie. "However, through experience, I've found something that keeps me anchored and helps me deal with situations. That something has been a total trust and reliance on God. I find that as I give over total control to God, things work out. I've had to make a commitment to daily prayer and time with God. That commitment is the key to learning trust. It's as if that time is my well from which I can draw strength."

Rosemarie still has hassles and challenges, information to gather and weigh, and tough decisions about her child to make. But trusting God has given her a strength that she doesn't have on her own and the peace that transcends understanding to deal with the present and face the future with hope.

Christian Support Groups

One of the distinctions of Christian support groups is prayer. "Our main purposes are to support, bless, and pray for each other, so we spend a lot of time doing just that!" says Julie Shanafelt. She and her husband, John, started a support group at Faith Community Church in The Woodlands, Texas, for parents whose children have all kinds of disabilities. The bimonthly group picks the subjects they want to deal with, and each meeting focuses on one issue—for example, how to handle meetings with teachers and other school staff, spiritual concerns for their children, disciplining their children, and how to make plans for their children's future. Sometimes they bring in a speaker (e.g., they invited the pastor to discuss spiritual concerns with them), and in other meetings they exchange ideas. They keep the group open to new parents and advertise the meetings in the church newsletter.

"We always go away encouraged, and we find the meetings when both parents can attend especially helpful," Julie says. "And when we see each other outside the meetings, we have an immediate connection and empathy for each other."

Mom's Night Out

Mothers of children with a variety of disabilities and special needs, ranging from ADD (attention deficit disorder) to cerebral palsy, from chronic illness to mental retardation, meet once a month at a restaurant in the Tulsa, Oklahoma, area. They start at 6:30 P.M. and may get home around midnight. These mothers eat and visit, occasionally gripe about doctors, and always exchange helpful information.

"It does more for me emotionally than anything else I do

throughout the month," says one mother. When she explains that her son is about to have surgery, the other moms understand her anxiety. They talk about school and IEP (individualized education plan) meetings. When a new mom comes, they get her plugged into community resources, newsletters, and other support. And most of all, they listen.

This type of support group is less structured than the kind the group's coordinator, Donna Johnson, was first involved with when her son was a year old and newly diagnosed with CP. At that time, she went to the local CP support group, where the focus was more on educating the parents within an eight-week time period. One week a counselor would speak about the stresses in marriage, and another week a speaker discussed different physical therapy approaches. The information they gained was valuable, "but there's a point at which you've got the information and you need a shoulder to cry on and someone to share experiences with," says Donna. This "Mom's Night Out" group fills that need for her and the other women who attend.

To announce the group's meetings, Donna sends out a mailer each month to all the families in the Special Friends Ministry of their church, telling them the place and time. They also reach out to mothers in the community who don't attend their church but have children with disabilities, and they're developing quite a network. Two of the mothers whose children died in the past year still come to the meetings because the fellowship is so supportive.

A Commitment to Change

Dani Steiger, a California mom, attends a support group for parents of children with special needs that meets in a local church. Dani's son, Daniel, has fragile X syndrome, which means he's easily distracted, has autistic tendencies, and is extremely sensitive to noises and crowds. "We pray before the meeting and truly support and love each other," Dani says. "Our focus is on the commitment to change and improve the situation, whatever it is, instead of wallowing in self-pity or turning into a groaning session." They have speakers at each meeting, and afterward the parents have coffee, talk, and share ideas.

"My favorite speaker was the head attorney of the Protection and Advocacy Center in California," says Dani. Listening to him gave Dani the courage to be the advocate her son needed in school matters. The support group is also where Dani heard about a terrific summer camp her son was eligible to attend and a support group for 8-to-12-year-old boys that a local psychologist was starting. There the counselor helped the boys deal with their anger and learn communication skills. "It helped Daniel to know that other kids get called names and have problems too, creating awareness that he's not the only one," says his mom.

"Special children are a challenge," adds Dani. "And when you've got other parents who hear your frustrations without hearing them as a burden, it's a relief. In addition, I always learn about resources I didn't know about. Or when a parent tells her story, I may get an idea for something that would help my son."

Dani has also found great help in the National Fragile X Foundation, and one of the best benefits is the team of experts it makes available to parents. The physicians who speak at the seminars include handouts with their phone numbers, so she can get an expert on the phone within just a few minutes. The foundation's newsletter includes articles by parents and doctors, features on new research, and stories about children with fragile X that are positive and give parents hope. All these resources are part of Dani's support system.

Where Can You Find a Support Group?

Where can you find a parent support group that will help you in the ways described above? Here are some ideas:

- Check with your local ARC (Association for Retarded Citizens) and MHMR (Mental Health and Mental Retardation) offices, which sponsor support groups for parents of children and adults with special needs.

- Check with Easter Seals, the local Cerebral Palsy Association, and chapters of any local support organizations. Some Easter Seals facilities have parent support groups available so that while children are in therapy, their parents can interact in a group setting without extra scheduling.

- Check with nearby children's hospitals, which often provide support groups. For example, Children's Hospital in our city has different groups for different special needs. One of these, called "Lifeline," is the support group for the parents of children who have had heart surgery or heart problems.

- Ask therapists, case managers, social workers, and your doctors for the names and phone numbers of coordinators of different groups. In addition, check with your school district's special education department for parent-to-parent groups.

- Check with the national organization of your child's disability to see if it can connect you with a local chapter.

- Call the offices of your church and other churches in your community to see if any Christian support groups are available.

- *Exceptional Parent* magazine and NATHHAN (National Challenged Homeschoolers Associated Network) connect parents as pen pals with other families with a child with a similar disability, providing extra support without having to leave your home. For *Exceptional Parent,* call (800) 247-8080 or (800) 562-1973, or contact the staff on the Internet at http://www.familyeducation.com. To contact NATHHAN, call (206) 857-4257 or E-mail: NATHANEWS@aol.com.

Above all, keep asking until you find a group that fits your needs.

Starting a Support Group

If a parent support group is not available in your community or church, or if you find that the existing ones don't meet your family's needs, consider *starting* a group. Here are some suggestions for an effective beginning:

1. Decide on your focus. When Marilyn Talmadge decided to start a support group for mothers of children with special needs in her church, she chose to be under the umbrella of their church's "friend-

ship groups" to benefit from the pastoral support. The group consists of 12 to 16 mothers at a time, and their purpose is clear: to encourage one another, pray and be there for each other, and help the church know how to respond to these parents and their children.

The women had enjoyed the friendship groups they'd attended in the past, but they felt the other people just couldn't relate to their struggles and didn't understand when they shared the needs of their children and how their lives were affected. "But in this group," says Marilyn, "when someone shares something, there's an instant, 'Oh yes! I've been there,' a real sense of camaraderie and understanding."

In addition, each of the women has been hurt at some time in the context of the church's response to her child's handicap, and one of Marilyn's goals is to form a channel that will reopen communication between the mothers and the church.

2. Call a few parents on the phone, or mail them a short letter. Tell them who you are, how you got their names, and that you're interested in starting a parent support group. If you're going to meet in homes, you could have your first meeting begin with a potluck in which each person brings a dish, or you could serve dessert and coffee during a get-acquainted time.

3. Try to meet without your children. If baby-sitting is a problem, check with different ladies' groups, school parent-teacher organizations, or church

groups. You may be surprised at the positive responses and offers of help you get after you explain what you're trying to do.

4. Decide whether the group is for moms, dads, or both, depending on the needs of the families and when the meetings are held. Some parents feel the best group is a combined group of moms and dads, because feelings can sometimes be expressed in group discussions that mates may not otherwise comprehend. If you decide to gather as moms only, it might be helpful to provide a separate time for the men to meet. One support group has the mothers meeting once a month and the dads meeting separately once a month, and then all the parents come together for a meal and meeting. Fathers need a place to express feelings, too, and can greatly benefit from the support of a group.

5. Don't spend all the time at every meeting discussing your children, says one veteran of parent support groups. Take time to do things before the group discussion, such as have a guest speaker, watch one family's silly home movie, or anything the group would like to do that will produce laughter. Have a game night or a barbecue for the parents and kids once in a while.

6. Find a facilitator. You might lead the group yourself. Some groups find it's helpful to have a social worker or psychologist to keep the group on track if conversation becomes very negative. Others have different parents sign up to facilitate each meeting.

They begin their times together by going around the room and having everyone respond to the same question (e.g., "What is your worst fear in having a special-needs child?" or "What's the biggest problem you've overcome or helped your child overcome?"). If you have a speaker, that person can lead the discussion after making his or her presentation. (*Our thanks to Louise Stewart and Donna Johnson for some of these tips on starting a support group.*)

Whether the group is structured or unstructured; whether it includes only moms or a mixed group of parents; whether it's held in your church or as part of an agency or children's hospital—being part of a parent support group can bring a sense of belonging, valuable information, and a network of friends who over time become almost as close as family.

Encouragement from Scripture

- "Be kind and compassionate to one another" (Ephesians 4:32).

- "I urge, then, first of all, that requests, prayers, intercession and thanksgiving be made for everyone" (1 Timothy 2:1).

- "I have never stopped thanking God for you. I pray for you constantly, asking God, the glorious Father of our Lord Jesus Christ, to give you wisdom to see clearly and really understand who Christ is and all that he has done for you" (Ephesians 1:16-17, TLB).

- "Do everything in love" (1 Corinthians 16:14).

- "Your care for others is the measure of your greatness" (Luke 9:48, TLB).

CHAPTER 4

FAITH OR FEAR: DEALING WITH ANXIETY

I (Louise) hung up the telephone with a sigh of relief. The speech pathologist was running 15 minutes late, giving me some much-needed time to get myself and Jay ready. We finally made it into the bathroom to brush his teeth when suddenly, the color drained from his face as he clutched his chest and fell forward into my arms. In an instant, my day went from "almost normal" to a slow-motion, adrenaline-pumping emergency.

Somehow I managed to get Jay to the sofa and call 911. My heart pounded, and I could hear the fear in my own voice as I quickly exclaimed, "My son has severe heart disease and has just passed out!" The words spilled out so quickly that the whole sentence sounded like one word. As I rushed to the bathroom for a damp cloth, the cardiologist's words hammered in my memory: "Jay is at great risk for a stroke or fatal cardiac arrhythmia." My hands shook as I bathed his pale face with the wet cloth and prayed silently, "Please, God, don't let him die!"

Just a few minutes earlier, I had been making plans to meet my husband for lunch while Jay spent a couple of hours with his speech pathologist. Now my mind was deluged with thoughts like *We didn't make it to the twentieth birthday after all.* This was to be his "miracle birthday," the birthday that doctors had never given us hope of seeing. The big party was only two weeks away. Now here we were, paramedics rushing in to try to save my son.

I stepped away as trained hands immediately went to work taking blood pressure, pulse, and oxygen saturation levels. An eternity seemed to pass. Finally, some color began to creep into Jay's face, and he was coherent enough to answer questions.

"Hey, buddy, can you tell me where you hurt?" the para- medic asked.

"Knee," Jay quickly responded, pointing to his left knee. He had accidentally banged his knee on the sofa as he rushed through the living room before brushing his teeth.

More questions followed. More answers came, even a giggle as the paramedic hit a ticklish spot during his exam. Within 15 minutes, the crisis had passed. It was determined that Jay had hit his knee hard enough to precipitate a vaso-vagal response, causing him to faint when his blood pressure took a sharp drop, a result of standing up too quickly with severe pain. Jay's doctor would confirm this diagnosis later. I breathed a silent prayer of thanks. No stroke. No fatal cardiac arrhyth- mia. No speeding ambulance rushing us to the hospital. We would see that twentieth birthday after all!

For some of us who have medically fragile children, this scene is all too common. In fact, too many times the gurney does not leave the house empty. Instead, an ambulance races the child to the hospital, where the parents sit by his side, hoping, praying, and wondering if this will be the last time they hold their child in their arms.

But on occasions, like that day, the results are good. And when the crisis has passed, we try to push the fear away from our consciousness. But just like a jack-in-the-box, wound up and ready to pop, that fear may lunge to the forefront with each subsequent crisis. We sometimes live in a world of free-floating anxiety.

It may be the kind of anxiety that floats in your stomach while you're waiting to see the dentist. Or it could be the worry over future problems, for we all wrestle that giant at times. Sometimes it's the kind of fear that suffocates. Your heart races, your hands shake, and your voice trembles. You feel light-headed, and your stomach turns cartwheels while you struggle for breath. That's panic! And it can happen in a moment.

From Panic to Peace

How do we turn this around? How do we go from panic to peace? We know how we got from peace to panic, but how do we reverse the process? Is it possible to let go of the image of a child falling limp into our arms, of a small body twisted with seizures, or of eyes reflecting pain? What about that raspy rattle of a child struggling for breath when her fragile body is ravaged by cystic fibrosis, pneumonia, asthma, chemotherapy, or any number of other illnesses?

How do we let go of these haunting thoughts and find peace? It's not that we aren't thankful for the good moments or for God's protection. In fact, we're so grateful that we may hover too closely and become overprotective parents. We fear any separation. Even letting our children ride in a car with someone else can become a struggle. After an extremely traumatic crisis, we put our child to bed with a prayer on our lips and fear in our hearts. We might even get up three or four times a night to make sure our precious child is still breathing.

One mother told me she sometimes sits beside her son's bed all night, just watching him sleep. That's thankfulness at its height—wanting to savor the very presence of your child. But it's also mixed with a fear that says, "What about the next time? Can I trust You, God?"

The good news is that panic is not the life God has called us to live. It's never His intention for us to live in constant fear. When Jesus said He would give us "the peace of God, which transcends all understanding" (Philippians 4:7), it included the assurance that our children are "safe" with Him. It's not a guarantee that everything will always turn out the way we want it to, but it does mean we will have *peace* no matter how many crises come into our lives.

New Year's Baby

Pam Whitley knows that peace, but she had to walk some anxious miles before finding it. At the age of 25, she was devastated by the death of her father and thought life could never again be completely fulfilling. But with time and the truth of Scripture, she began to experience God's peace concerning her father's passing. Soon Pam and her husband, Mike, along with their three-year-old son, moved into a new home. They had a wonderful Christmas as they awaited the birth of their second child. On January 1, they became the proud parents of Oklahoma City's first baby of the new year, a beautiful little girl they named Jan. Life was again close to perfect.

Only eight days later, however, Pam and Mike sat in a makeshift waiting area at Children's Hospital while their baby underwent emergency heart surgery. Pam had first noticed Jan's feet were purple and had thought her booties were too tight. But almost immediately, the rest of Jan's body began to turn a dusky gray, and she struggled for breath as her parents raced her to the hospital in the ice and snow. A heart catheterization was performed, followed by emergency surgery.

Now they waited—one hour, then two. The prognosis for this surgery was good, provided there were no surprises. But Jan was so tiny. Another hour dragged by. Outside, the cold January wind howled and blew through cracks in the flimsy walls of the waiting area under construction. Pam's fears mounted, and she pulled her coat closer to ward off the chill both inside and outside her body. Her breast milk began to leak through her clothes. She felt that her whole body was weeping for her baby.

Finally, after four hours, the surgeon appeared. Jan had survived the surgery. *However . . .* The word seemed to hang in the air. Jan had quit breathing during the surgery and had had to be resuscitated. Her body and brain had gone without oxygen for about 15 minutes. No one knew at that time what the outcome would be, but they would find out later that the little girl who was born on New Year's Day was gone forever. In her place was a severely brain-damaged child who would struggle all her life with constant seizures, high temperatures, and life-threatening infections. She would never walk, talk, or even use her hands.

God's Promises

Right away, Pam learned that her strength lay in prayer and the promises of God. She would continually pray God's Word over her child. And when times were so hard that she didn't know what to pray, when Jan suffered for days and nights without end, Pam prayed for mercy and mirrored scriptures back to the Lord, reminding Him of His promises.

"I believe in the sovereignty of God," says Pam, "and I know He has a plan and purpose for each person's life. I know He could have intervened and prevented Jan's brain damage, but I don't believe He caused it or intended it. In fact, I believe Jesus weeps when I weep. And these children, these special angels who have broken bodies or minds, will be among those in the highest positions in eternity."

This is a family that has been through the fire and come out with a stronger faith than they had when they began. It's the kind of faith God gives those who are tested, such as He gave to Job. It's a seeker's faith, as promised in Jeremiah 29:11-13: "'For I know the plans I have for you,' declares the LORD, '. . . plans to give you hope and a future. Then you will call upon me and come and pray to me, and I will listen to you. You will seek me and find me when you seek me with all your heart.'" This is no wimpy, pie-in-the-sky hope. This is a promise! This is for those who need "combat faith" in the heat of the battle. And for many parents, like Pam, the battle is for their children. It's in this arena where we find the real champions for God—the true seekers after His heart.

Jan is now 18 years old and still cannot walk, talk, or use her hands. But she can smile. And through her life and Pam's personal testimony, many people have trusted in the Lord as their Savior. Pam would never say her life has been easy, but she claims the joy of the Lord for her strength. And Jan continues to glorify God each day of her life, because her parents believe that God is still sovereign and will always bring good out of any situation.

How Pam mirrored scriptures back to God

- "Thank You, God, that You can and will supply all of *Jan's* needs, according to Your riches in glory by Christ Jesus" (Philippians 4:19).

- "And even the very hairs of *Jan's* head are all numbered. So don't be afraid; you, *Jan,* are worth more than many sparrows" (Matthew 10:30-31).

- "Thank You, Father, that You have given Your angels charge over *Jan* to guard *her* in all *her* ways" (Psalm 91:11).

Chapter 8 discusses in more detail how to pray for your child and yourself.

More Grace

Prayer brings peace. Prayer also brings healing—sometimes to the body, but always to the heart and soul. And the secret to prayer is found in the Bible. It tells us how and when to pray.

Jesus taught His disciples to pray, "Our Father which art in heaven, Hallowed be thy name. Thy kingdom come. Thy will be done in earth, as it is in heaven. Give us this day our daily bread. And forgive us our debts, as we forgive our debtors. And lead us not into temptation, but deliver us from evil: For thine is the kingdom, and the power, and the glory, for ever. Amen" (Matthew 6:9-13, KJV).

As parents, we can apply the Lord's Prayer to our own unique circumstances:

- "Father, give both of us strength for daily therapies."

- "Forgive me for getting angry when someone stares and makes hurtful remarks, and forgive the person who offended my child and me."

- "Deliver me from the temptation to have a pity party when I'm tired."

- "Help me to remember that I am filled with Your power forever and ever."

When are we to pray? Paul told us in 1 Thessalonians 5:17, "Pray continually." That doesn't mean we're to be on our knees constantly, but we should be able to carry on a "continuous conversation" with our Father in heaven.

Barbara Lumpkin is another mother who found strength in prayer, especially in learning to pray continually. When her son, Richey, was diagnosed with Duchenne muscular dystrophy at four and one-half years of age, Barbara spent hours every day calling people, writing letters, and poring over medical books, looking for even a single sentence that was positive about the disease. "I just wanted it to say that in *some* cases this fatal diagnosis doesn't prove true," she says. "But it didn't happen. Everything was negative."

Barbara then went into depression, and she and her husband, Gary, found themselves accepting the grim prognosis that their only child would never live beyond his twelfth birthday. They tailored all their activities around this statistic, seldom leaving him except for business obligations. They wanted to have no regrets about how they had spent their parenting time if something happened.

And something did happen. Barbara discovered that statistics mean little and doctors are sometimes wrong. Richey not only saw his twelfth birthday, but at the time of this writing he's eagerly awaiting his *sixteenth*. And except for cruising in a wheelchair, he is extremely healthy and shows no signs of slowing down. He bowls weekly, sings in the youth choir at church, and belongs to a drama club for disabled people.

At the same time, Barbara has discovered the secret to peace in her life. "I try to stay in a prayerful state," she says. "It's like I carry on a conversation with my best friend throughout the day." And what if God doesn't heal Richey? "If there is one thing I have learned, it's that God gives *more grace* than I need. Not just enough or adequate, but always *more grace*. Some parents have to contend with their children getting into immoral lifestyles. I will never have to worry about that. And I take great comfort in knowing that Richey will never be on drugs or in jail or anything like that. He will just be in the arms of Jesus."

Faith Versus Fear

If prayer is the answer to panic, then faith must surely be the prescription for fear. And when are we more vulnerable than when our children are at risk? Candy Snowbarger has firsthand experience. When her seventh child was born, her first girl, she hardly had time to celebrate before she was told the baby had Down syndrome. And even before she could digest that information, little Sherah turned blue from low oxygen levels and had to be airlifted to a hospital in Wichita, Kansas.

"I had only held her one time and had to stay in the hospital because of having a C-section," says Candy. "All I could do was cry. I was in shock and couldn't even pray."

When Candy's pastor arrived, he began thanking God for all things—for a child with special needs, for medical bills their insurance wouldn't cover, and even for Sherah's heart condition that God could heal. "I knew he was right in giving thanks," Candy says, "but I felt like God had finally given me a daughter and then taken her away. I had no idea what to expect or what she would be like."

Finally, on day five, Sherah's oxygen saturation levels stabilized, and Candy was able to be alone with her baby for the first time since her birth. "When I changed her diaper, it hit me that I really had a girl, after six boys. And when she looked at me with those sweet, little, almond-shaped eyes, I just fell in love with her. I said, 'You are my daughter!' I realized that she still had our genes and was *like* us. She just got too much of a good thing (an extra twenty-first chromosome). At that moment, I began to experience joy and to accept her for the way God made her. That night, we put a headband on her, took pictures, and started having fun!"

Not all of Candy's fears are dissolved, however. Sherah still has heart surgery in her future. "I know I can trust God with her," Candy says, "but it's hard to put her in the hands of man." Candy relies strongly on prayer and leans on the prayers of others as well.

What are your fears and anxieties?

- Child's fragile health or future medical treatment?

- The future—the unknown. What will happen to him/her?

- Will my child have friends at school, at church, in the neighborhood?

- Can I juggle all the therapies and doctor visits and still keep a normal lifestyle for my family?

- What about finances?

- Can I trust God with my child?

You can probably think of a dozen more that are unique to your situation. How do you handle *your* fear and anxiety?

Too Young to Die

All parents of seriously ill children have one thing in common—they don't want their child to die prematurely. So how do parents handle the prospect that they will most likely outlive their child? What about ongoing grief? How do you let go? Following are some suggestions from parents of medically fragile children:

- Try to celebrate each day rather than dwelling on a negative prognosis.

- Respect and understand the information given to you by doctors, but realize that they don't always know what will happen.

- Remember that God loves you, and He loves your child even more than you do, even though that seems an impossibility.

God's Handiwork

Needles and hospitals are terrifying to Jay, so he screamed "No, no," as I (Louise) held him on my lap. He was about six years old and had developed a rash that caused the doctors to suspect bacterial endocarditis. Since this is a serious condition, we were immediately sent to the hospital for tests. Three blood draws had to be taken from Jay's arm at 30-minute intervals. The more he protested, the closer I held him and whispered over and over, "I love you, darlin'. Mommy loves you."

When the nurse finished the blood draw, I let go of him, expecting him to jump off my lap and run away. Instead, however, he turned and threw his arms around my neck, saying in his own way, "I love you, Mommy." He didn't understand my part in his pain, but he never doubted my love for a minute. Oh, that I trusted my heavenly Father the way Jay trusts me! Then when problems come, I would run into His arms and be comforted with His gentle whisper, "I love you, darlin'. I love you."

- Pray for a miracle, and remember that God is sovereign no matter what happens.

- Allow yourself to grieve at intervals, but don't live in constant grief or you'll miss the joy God sends through your child.

- Protect your child from illnesses and dangerous situations as much as possible, but don't smother her with your own fear.

One of the greatest things parents can do is to help their child develop a deep spiritual life. Read Scripture to him, pray with him, play Christian music, watch Christian videos or TV programs, talk with him, and answer any questions he might have about heaven or dying. As you dispel your child's fear, you also release your own.

If you're the parent of a medically fragile child, you may be experiencing anger, resentment, and bitterness. If so, immerse yourself in Scripture. Do an in-depth study of heaven and of God's glorious love. Joni Eareckson Tada's book *Heaven* is an excellent reference. When heaven and God's glory become real in your own life, you're better able to release your child to a loving heavenly Father.

Even if your child is unable to ask questions or understand deep spiritual concepts, he still understands the love of Jesus and will enjoy Christian music and Scripture. His heart is very tender, and he may have a deep longing to see Jesus. Allow him to foster that same longing in your own spirit—a burning desire to see Jesus in your daily life and then face to face in heaven.

The Security of Release

Twenty-five years ago, Robert and Judy Stipe became the parents of a son with special needs. "We knew absolutely nothing about cerebral palsy," says Judy, "but we were about to learn. Acceptance of Wesley's condition was not easy and didn't happen overnight. But when I gave Wesley's life to God and quit trying to do everything myself, things began to change."

How did Judy learn to release her anxiety and let God take over? "One day I mentally pictured Wesley in my hands, with me lifting him up and laying him in God's lap. I said, 'God, he is *Your* child, not mine. I only have him for a little while. Please help me to make the most of his time here.' God gave me a peace that is hard to explain. It grows daily as I release Wes to Him."

Through the years, Judy has practiced releasing her child to God daily: "Since I learned to 'Let go and let God,' there has been a daily filling of peace as I release each day's problems. My purpose is to pray daily for Wes and to have him anywhere

God wants to use him." And God definitely uses him. People tell Judy that Wes has ministered to them with only a smile. A child in her church told his mother that Jesus told him to pray for Wes. "I wish everyone, especially adults, could have the tender heart of a child toward one who is disabled," says Judy. "We can only wonder how many lives would be different."

Perhaps you would like to practice Judy's way of releasing your child to God. Picture a loving, heavenly Father holding your precious child in His lap. Can you envision anything more beautiful? Now, let go and let God give you peace!

Special Stress Stoppers

Whether you fear a health, emotional, or financial crisis, you may want to try some of these practical tips:

- Avoid isolation! Talk with another parent or close friend who will let you express your feelings without being judgmental. Join a support group.

- Write out your thoughts and feelings—anger, fear, guilt, and so on. Try writing a letter to God.

- Educate yourself on your child's disability. Information relieves stress.

- Do something for someone else. Nothing takes your mind off your own problems like doing something for another person. Visit a shut-in, water plants for a neighbor on vacation, or do some other act of kindness.

- Meditate on Scripture. Write out verses on small note cards, and carry them in your purse or pocket so you can pray over them when you have a free moment.

- Listen to music. Praise tapes are wonderful for lifting your spirits. Instrumentals help soothe frazzled nerves.

- Ask for help! This sounds simple, but most of us don't like to ask. And *never* turn down offered help.

- Don't beat up on yourself when you make mistakes. Throw guilt in the gutter, where it belongs.

- Take care of yourself. If you don't take care of your own health, you can't take care of your child.

- Make life as simple as possible. Don't assume you have to do everything according to the "norm." If your child has trouble with shoelaces, buy shoes with Velcro! The key is to adapt.

- Learn to laugh! It's medicinal. Proverbs 17:22 says, "A cheerful heart is good medicine, but a crushed spirit dries up the bones."

- Purchase a pager or cellular phone if you have a medically fragile child. "The peace of mind I received in knowing that I could be reached at any time was well worth the monthly fee," says Dottie Young, mother of Katie, who has Rett syndrome.

Lighter Side

Valerie Campbell is a self-professed worrier. "Even as a child, I would find something to worry about," she says. "It became a way of life." Now, with a son who has Williams syndrome and heart disease, her worry can easily get out of control. But her husband, Dale, is a great stress-buster. Valerie relates the tremendous anxiety she faced when their son, Brian, was going into his first surgery.

"We knew absolutely no one in the town and had no support system," she reports. "It was just the two of us! It was overwhelming when they placed Brian, just a tiny baby, on that giant gurney. Dale patted me and said, 'Now, don't worry. Everything will be fine. Didn't you see those two big angels with Brian? One of them was so big he hit his wing on the way out the door!'"

Dale's support and humor have helped Valerie through subsequent surgeries for Brian and other stressful times. "When you laugh," Valerie says, "it diffuses a lot of the anxiety."

Encouragement from Scripture

- "May God bless you richly and grant you increasing freedom from all anxiety and fear" (1 Peter 1:2, TLB).

- "Have I not commanded you? Be strong and courageous. Do not be terrified; do not be discouraged, for the LORD your God will be with you wherever you go" (Joshua 1:9).

- "You saw me before I was born and scheduled each day of my life before I began to breathe. Every day was recorded in your Book!" (Psalm 139:16, TLB). (Remember this when doctors give a bleak prognosis and you are paralyzed with fear. Your child's life is in God's hands. Don't let fear of the unknown steal your joy or rob you of hope.)

- "I can do everything God asks me to with the help of Christ who gives me the strength and power" (Philippians 4:13, TLB).

- "When you lie down, you will not be afraid; when you lie down, your sleep will be sweet" (Proverbs 3:24). (What a precious promise for parents who are physically and emotionally exhausted!)

- "Let him have all your worries and cares, for he is always thinking about you and watching everything that concerns you" (1 Peter 5:7, TLB).

- "Jehovah himself is caring for you!" (Psalm 121:5, TLB).

- "You will keep in perfect peace him whose mind is steadfast, because he trusts in you" (Isaiah 26:3).

- "For God hath not given us the spirit of fear; but of power, and of love, and of a sound mind" (2 Timothy 1:7, KJV). (If you're prone to panic, keep this verse right up front in your memory bank, and use it often.)

The Psalms are an ideal place to run when you're fearful or anxious. Try reading a favorite psalm and saying, "Lord, this is exactly how I feel. Would You accept this as my prayer?" God will always be faithful to do exactly that.

You may even want to write out your own psalm. Along with your petition to God, be sure to include praise and thanksgiving for the answer He will send.

CHAPTER 5

BECOMING AN EXPERT ON YOUR CHILD

Tim and Tammy Townsend nervously seated themselves at the table with the rest of the multidisciplinary team from their daughter's early-intervention program, wondering why the school had requested this meeting. "There were about 10 people there," says Tammy, "and I was scared to death. They already considered me an overprotective mom, so I didn't know what to expect. I was also pretty insecure and had told them I wasn't a teacher or therapist; I was just Brittany's mom."

Tim smiled at two-and-a-half-year-old Brittany, seated on his lap, and gave her an affectionate squeeze. She looked up at her daddy and laughed. "Suddenly, there was total silence in the room," said Tammy. "Everyone was staring at us with mouth open, and I thought, *What? Are we holding her wrong?* It was very uncomfortable."

Finally, one of the team members spoke up: "How do you get her to smile and laugh and interact like that? We haven't been able to get her to respond to anything."

The teachers explained how they had tried everything they knew, but that Brittany, who would later be diagnosed with Rett syndrome, withdrew from everyone.

Tim and Tammy described how Brittany smiled, laughed, and gave lots of hugs and kisses at home. The team was amazed and eager to know how to interact with Brittany.

"At the meeting, I realized that *I* was the expert on Brittany," says Tammy. "Even though I didn't know anything about therapy or teaching, I knew how to love Brittany, and that was what she needed most." Tammy was able to explain special ways to love and relate to her daughter to the team, and Brittany soon began to respond to her teachers.

The Real Expert

Like Tammy, many parents mistakenly believe that professionals know more about their children than they do. Granted, teachers may have teaching techniques you don't know. Doctors will be able to diagnose and treat illnesses that you aren't equipped to handle. But you, the parent, are the *real expert* on your child. You're the one feeding him, nurturing him, praying for him, and tucking him into bed at night. You eventually learn every little thing about your child.

When our children are babies, we come to recognize their cries and know immediately from the sound or intensity if they are hungry, hurting, or just want to be held. In the same way, we parents of children with special needs can study our kids and learn their likes, dislikes, actions, reactions, mannerisms, gestures—everything about them. This knowledge will be useful not only in a practical sense while caring for them at home, but it will also provide valuable insight when dealing with professional people in our children's lives.

There are numerous ways to become an expert on your child, but there's no "perfect formula." Many parents, however, have found the suggestions in this chapter to be extremely helpful.

Seek God's Guidance

One of the first things I (Louise) learned to do as a new mom, feeling inadequate and isolated, was to ask God for wisdom and guidance. There were no infant stimulation programs, and I had no one to advise me, so I relied on God's direction. Even with early intervention programs and support groups now available, prayer is still a great source of strength. No matter how much knowledge you gain or how many people are supporting you, nothing can replace the knowledge and help that come from talking daily with your heavenly Father.

Educate Yourself

Read books, pamphlets, articles, medical journals—everything available on your child's disability. Contact national organizations to get valuable information on research, reading lists, books, and medical breakthroughs, as well as monthly newsletters. Some examples of national organizations are: Williams Syndrome Association, Fragile X Foundation, Down Syndrome Congress, United Cerebral Palsy Foundation, Easter Seals Society, NICHY (National Information Center for Handicapped Children and Youth), and the National Parent Network on Disabilities. (See the resources section at the end of this book for a more complete list of organizations.)

Several magazines are targeted to the parents of children with special needs as well, including *Special Education Today* and *Special Family. Exceptional Parent* magazine covers a multitude of disabilities as well as adaptive equipment and where it can be purchased.

Find out about organizations in your own state, too. Most states have a central number that can give you information on a variety of disabilities. For instance, in Oklahoma you can contact OASIS, and the people there will connect you with an organization for a particular disability or give you the information you need. You can even gain valuable information from newsletters. Most will list seminars and workshops offered in your area. Our state holds an annual governor's conference on people with disabilities. Call your state government to see if one is offered in your state. You can also get in touch with a parent who has learned to advocate for her child and request information on organizations from her. And don't forget your local library. Not only will you find books and magazines there, but you may also be able to use the computer to get on the Internet and find valuable information about organizations, hospitals, and so on across the nation.

One couple called all over the country until they found a hospital that was doing research on their child's illness. Then they called the researcher. That call resulted in a lung transplant for their baby that saved her life.

To discover what's available locally, call the office of handicapped concerns, department of human services, state department of education, Easter Seals, your local ARC (Association for Retarded Citizens), or the national organization for your own child's disability. They can connect you with a local chapter. Or ask your child's doctors, therapists, and teachers, as well as other parents, for information. If there's a teaching hospital in your vicinity, ask to use its library for referral to local groups and programs. Many of these hospitals also have child study centers that offer information and even therapy to qualified individuals.

Some colleges and universities also offer helpful programs. (Most have long waiting lists, so put your child's name on the list when he or she is an infant.) One university in our area provides a preschool for children with special needs. It also has a "special buddies" program for adults who are developmentally disabled.

Keep a Balance

As important as gathering information is, be careful to keep a balance in your life. Become and remain an informed parent, but don't make the pursuit of knowledge your main goal. Search out the program that will help your child develop to his or her highest potential. That could be the first program you observe or the tenth.

Bonnie Shepherd tells how she became obsessed with gaining knowledge when her son, Adam, was born: "I would go to the library and find everything I could and ask friends who were doctors to do the same in their medical libraries." She then made a list of possible resources and placed it in the public library for other parents. Although she gained valuable information about her son's disability, she found that her expertise actually worked to her disadvantage at times.

"I would go into a doctor's office, and when we talked he would think, *Oh, here's someone with knowledge, so I can talk to her on a different level.* Then the doctor missed the personal side of what was going on with my child. And I was doing this intellectual exercise and discussing physiology when I probably needed to know more practical, day-to-day information."

And all the information Bonnie received still didn't answer the basic questions in her heart: "Why did this happen to my child?" and "Did I do something wrong in my pregnancy?"

"I may never know what caused Adam's disability," she says, "but I *do* need to know how to become an expert on raising my child." So she shifted her focus to doing things that were important at the moment—practical things like therapy and networking with other parents of children with special needs to find programs, or even creating them if nothing was available.

Bonnie still recommends that parents gain a thorough knowledge of their child's disability, but her definition of becoming an expert is that parents recognize the subtle little things about their child that other people won't pick up. "I realized I needed to be really tuned in to Adam's needs and know how to meet them," she says.

Quiz the Doctors

To gain greater understanding of your child's disability, quiz the doctors. In the words of one dad, "Question the doctors until they're tired of answering." Of course, that's extreme, but the message is clear: Ask, ask, ask! You will never learn what you need to know about your child's disability unless you ask. Don't just stick to general questions about your child's health, either. Ask the probing questions that haunt you day and night, such as:

- How many children have this disability?

- What is my child's life expectancy?

- Have you ever treated children with this disorder?

- What can I do at home to help my child?

- Is this hereditary?

- Why did this happen?

- What treatment is available?

Deep inside, you may even be asking, "Can you fix what's wrong with my child?" But whatever your questions, make a list of them. Ask about anything that bothers you. *You need information*. Without it, you can become anxious and upset. With it, you can have more peace of mind and choose the treatment and programs that will best help your child.

Martha New kept a log of things that were happening at home when she and her husband, Bayne, were searching for a diagnosis for their daughter, Jennifer. "It's very useful when you go to the doctor," Bayne observed. "You can say, 'She does *this* at *these* times.'" They learned that the more specific they could be about their daughter's behavior, the better their chance of getting an accurate diagnosis. It would also be beneficial to keep a log of your child's medications and her reactions.

Find Positive Doctors

It's vital that you choose physicians in whom you have confidence and with whom you enjoy open communication. A good dose of optimism is also beneficial. Even with the worst diagnosis, a doctor should never destroy a parent's hope. After all, only God knows the ultimate outcome.

Understand, however, that the doctor may be trying to avoid giving you unrealistic expectations. It's his job to diagnose and treat your child's illness or disability, and he's probably doing the best he can. But it's also his responsibility to give you the information you need to become an informed and involved parent. Physicians, therapists, and parents need to work as a team to provide the best plan of care for your child. Never underestimate your importance on the team. Your input and insight are vital!

Stephanie Alexander is adamant about having positive doctors around her daughter, Audrey, who has spina bifida. Audrey sees a neurosurgeon, orthopedic surgeon, and a urologist, along with the pediatrician for normal childhood illnesses.

"Going to the doctors' offices can wear on you mentally, so we surround ourselves with specialists who make us feel they truly care about Audrey," Stephanie says. "They focus on her, smile at her, maybe even hold her." At one point Stephanie changed doctors, driving three hours every three months so Audrey could be treated by a physician who believed she would walk rather than one who held little hope. "It was worth it," says Stephanie, "and Audrey is walking!"

At three and a half years old, Audrey has had four surgeries and numerous renal studies, but she loves her doctors. "If the physician doesn't have a happy attitude about your child, it would be worthwhile to look for someone else," Stephanie concludes.

Louise Stewart echoes the same advice. Her son, Patrick, had seen 15 different doctors by the end of his first year. "If you have chosen a physician you're unhappy with, don't stay with him because you feel intimidated," Louise counsels. "You must have a completely open relationship with your child's physicians. Why stay with a doctor who has bad bedside manners when there are other highly skilled doctors in the same field who know how to make parents feel like they're part of the team?"

While Patrick was in the hospital, Louise became frustrated

with his orthopedic surgeon and the physical therapist who insisted that one of Patrick's legs was shorter than the other. The therapist fit him in braces that had one raised shoe. Louise had such a bad feeling about the therapy that she asked the doctor to take new X rays to confirm the length of each leg. The doctor denied the request, barred her from Patrick while he was in therapy, and then refused further discussion.

Since Patrick had a night pass to sleep at home, Louise took her son out of the hospital that evening and never returned. While reading an old medical article, she found the name of an orthopedic doctor who was a specialist in his field and treated children's defects similar to Patrick's. She switched doctors and later learned that she had been exactly right—Patrick's legs were the same length, and the braces and shoe lift could have caused severe spinal damage if worn for an extended time.

Although Louise didn't find a miracle cure with the new physician, a heavy weight was lifted from her shoulders. The confidence and trust she felt with him were a great relief. By this doctor's request, her son began to work with several therapists regularly, which further improved his physical development.

Changing Negative to Positive

Unfortunately, with today's managed health care, you may not have the option of choosing your physician, especially when a specialist is needed. Your primary care physician will make the recommendation. Ask to have as much input as possible in choosing the physician, however; then make the best of the situation.

Just before Jay was born, my (Louise's) long-trusted pediatrician brought his son into practice with him. Since his son had special training with newborns, our doctor felt his son should be Jay's primary pediatrician. I wasn't convinced, since the elder doctor had managed to keep my two older children healthy. Reluctantly I agreed, however, and much to my pleased surprise, Jay received excellent care.

A few years later, the young doctor moved out of state. Soon after that, the elder doctor retired, leaving two associates I had hardly seen. In domino fashion, the associate I felt most comfortable with joined a private insurance group, and I was left with only one doctor who had ever treated Jay. As if that wasn't bad enough, this doctor seemed annoyed with all the questions I asked.

Finally I asserted myself and said, "I have the right to ask these questions, and you have an obligation to answer them." I let him know I was *not* questioning his ability as a physician or his integrity, but I needed to be an informed parent, and he needed my input.

Having cleared the air, we eventually became a team, and he is still Jay's primary physician. He and Jay have a great relationship and give each other a "high five" when they meet. Knowing how conscientious I am about Jay's health, he now looks to me for necessary information. His whole staff realizes that my call could be an emergency, and they respond promptly when I call with a health concern. The physician is also careful about Jay's suppressed immune system. Recently, on a "well checkup," he ushered us out the back door so Jay would not be exposed to any illnesses in the waiting room.

The bottom line is that if the relationship with your child's physician starts out rocky, it can turn around *if* the doctor truly cares about your child and is willing to listen to you. But if the doctor is uncaring, rude, or doesn't treat your child with dignity and respect, do whatever it takes to find another physician!

Children Teach Doctors

A new program for pediatric residents is emerging in a few teaching hospitals around the country. Doctors are again making house calls, but for a new reason. They're learning what it means to discharge a chronically ill child from the hospital—what special equipment is needed in the home, how the family lifestyle changes, and the medical procedures parents must learn to perform at home.

The program is called DOCC (Delivery of Chronic Care). The goal is to teach new pediatricians that their patient is a *child*, not just a set of symptoms, and that it's their obligation to understand how much they can and should help the child and the family. With only one house call, a physician begins to see what a child is like as a part of his or her home and family, not just as a patient. (See the resource section for more information on DOCC.)

Tips for Visiting the Doctor's Office

- Keep a notebook or journal of your child's medical history, development, and any specific behaviors that could be useful for the physician to know about. Include medications, allergies, and reactions. One mom even used a picture album to show her daughter's regression. It helped the professionals determine a diagnosis.

- Educate yourself on your child's disability or illness with medical books and articles written for lay people so you can ask questions.

- Write out your questions. In the stress or rush of the appointment, you might forget something important if you don't have it written out.

- Take pen and paper for note taking. Ask the doctor to repeat or reword anything you don't understand. If necessary, ask for permission to record the conversation.

- Allow yourself time to make well-thought-out decisions. Only in an emergency should you have to make hasty decisions.

- If you're concerned about a treatment your child is receiving and want the doctor to really listen to you, back up your thoughts and feelings with facts. For instance, if you're concerned about dosage on a medication, note the time medication was given, when it wore off, and any reactions your child experienced. This gives you factual data to support your anxiety and questions.

- If your child is having surgery, ask the doctor if he performs this surgery often. Make sure each of your child's doctors is a pediatric specialist, including the anesthesiologist. Be aware that doctors must inform you of all risk factors. You may also ask the percentages of each risk occurring and which dangers the doctor has personally seen develop. Finally, ask what the physician's personal recommendation would be.

- Prepare your child ahead of time for a visit to the doctor or hospital, letting him or her know what to expect. For instance, you might choose not to allow injections on "well checkups." That way, your child is never stressed about going. If immunizations need to be updated, make a separate trip, with the child already prepared. Of course, you can't make such promises on "sick" visits.

Gaining Knowledge Through Other Parents

Another way to gain knowledge about your child's disability is through support groups (see chapter 3) and other parents. It's always a blessing when you find another parent who has been where you're going or is traveling right beside you. You can gain practical information from such a person and possibly find a different way to solve a problem.

Debra Venard and Gayla Syed met at a Buddy Walk, which was held for Down syndrome awareness. Both had little girls with Down syndrome, and the moms bonded immediately.

"We pump each other up," says Gayla, who describes herself as having an easygoing, laid-back personality.

"We're opposites in one respect, but we complement each other," says Debra, who tends to be compulsive. "We're both very positive-minded, face some of the same problems, and are on the same level spiritually. I think that's what makes us a unique pair."

The team of two is obviously working. Before the next annual Buddy Walk, both moms were invited to a local Christian radio station, where they not only gave the specifics of the coming event but were also able to talk about acceptance, awareness, and their faith. They received a call on the program from someone who had just met a mom of a child with Down syndrome the day before. She was eager to pass on the information that Debra and Gayla gave in the interview.

Besides learning from each other, parents can also offer encouragement, exchange information, and even trade baby-sitting. If you don't know another parent with a situation similar to yours, ask your child's therapists and doctors, friends, and church members, or just take the initiative when you see another mom in a store. There's usually a kinship between parents of children with special needs, and who knows, you just might meet your new best friend in a checkout lane at Wal-Mart!

Assert Yourself

A parent is the child's strongest advocate in every situation, even in medical issues, so you need to learn early how to assert yourself with grace and dignity. You may have to speak up when it isn't comfortable or fight battles when you don't feel like fighting. But remember, *you're* the expert on your child.

Debbie Jeffers had never considered herself an advocate, but when the insurance company refused to pay for testing for her daughter's diagnosis, she got angry. Ashlee has Ring 22, a rare chromosome disorder with only 40 documented cases. Four of those cases are in the United States, and each is unique. "I had nothing to go on to learn about my child," says Debbie. "I had to start from scratch."

When the insurance company wanted to stick a label on Ashlee without a clear diagnosis, Debbie stepped in. "How could they treat my child if they didn't know what was wrong with her?" she says. She wrote letters to the insurance commissioner, as well as to the top executives of her husband's company. Within nine months, the insurance company paid for testing for Ashlee. When Ring 22 was diagnosed, they also paid for Debbie's testing to see if she was a carrier.

Psychological Evaluations and Testing

Before entering a program and every three years thereafter in most cases, your child will be evaluated by a psychologist or school psychometrist. Most ask that the parents not be present in the room while the child is being tested, assuming he or she will perform better alone. You know your child better than the person doing the testing, however. If you feel strongly that your child will perform better with you present, then politely insist.

It's extremely important that parents of a child who is non-verbal or has limited verbal skills be allowed to view their child's evaluation process. Also, before the evaluation, ask for an explanation of the testing instrument that will be used. Some tests penalize a child who has limited verbal skills, and the parent can request a different one. You can even request an independent evaluation if you don't feel the school psychometrist has tested your child fairly.

Because of Jay's limited communication, I (Louise) always sit in on his testing. He feels much more confident just having me there. I don't interfere with the testing, but I have an understanding with the examiner ahead of time that if she doesn't understand Jay's speech, she can glance at me and I will shake my head yes or no to let her know if his answer is right. She can proceed with the testing without interruption. There are also times when I *know* he knows an answer but doesn't understand the question because of the way it's worded. I ask if she can word the question differently. Some testing instruments are very structured and don't allow the examiner to change the question. Others offer the examiner more leeway.

Even if the test prevents rewording the question, a psychologist may do so just for the sake of finding the child's actual knowledge. This won't help the child's test score, but it builds his confidence for the next question and lets both you and the examiner know things that can't be put on paper. And with that knowledge, you can work toward helping the child understand questions worded in different ways.

The bottom line on being present during an evaluation is this: If the examiner knows she will have your support and cooperation, there should be no problem with your presence. Also, act in your child's best interest. Be present if you feel he will perform better with you there, but wait outside the room if you think otherwise.

Learn to Communicate

Your child's greatest challenge may be communication. It's important to provide him or her with any means of communication that work. Even though Jay comprehends speech and questions that are addressed to him, he finds it difficult to respond due to a severe speech articulation disorder, so he began sign language when he was very young. Most speech pathologists will tell you that the hands are usually easier to manipulate than the tongue and mouth, which makes signing an accessible language.

Some children, however, won't be able to speak *or* sign. In that case, the parent may have to rely on facial expressions, different sounds from the child, or even eye blinks. Some are able to use computers that are facilitated by eye movement or head wands. Jay now has an augmentative speech communication device that consists of a laptop computer with a voice synthesizer and touch screen. He can even choose the type of voice he wants to speak his message and can now say complete sentences that were once impossible.

When Jay was using sign language, he would sometimes want

to tell me (Louise) a word that he didn't have in his vocabulary. He would grab the signing dictionary and plop it in my hands as if to say, "Look it up so I can say what I want to say!" The problem was, I didn't know what to look up. But with gestures, pointing, words, and even charades of sorts, he always got his message across.

If your child's receptive ability is greater than his expressive language, you will have to educate others. If people can't understand a child's speech, they usually assume the child can't understand them either. To prevent your child from being ignored, bring him into the conversation.

At restaurants, for example, if the waiter asks me what Jay wants, I turn to him and ask what he wants. If the waiter doesn't understand, I translate, but at least Jay is given the independence of speaking for himself. This helps build self-esteem and keeps him from withdrawing due to poor communication skills.

You can also get lightweight, portable speech devices that can be programed with limited words for such things as restaurants, ball games, church, and so on. The parent or caregiver can insert a small number of comments in the device, such as "I'd like a hamburger, french fries, and Coke, please," or "I need to use the restroom." At the touch of a button, the person using the device can assert some independence in his life. One can also use picture cards in the same way. Your speech pathologist should be able to help you find a good form of communication.

Instruct close friends and extended family members in how your child communicates so they will feel comfortable speaking to him. Even if they still don't understand your child, assure them that he enjoys the conversation and interaction.

Choosing Child Care

Finding in-home care for a person with special needs can be difficult, especially for one who is medically fragile, or for a teenager or adult who is developmentally disabled. Even if you have family or friends to help you, there will be times when you'll need to hire someone. Look for a mature, responsible person, preferably one trained in CPR. Several agencies train people to become habilitation specialists. The department of human services can probably give you a list of agencies. These individuals are required to have Red Cross and CPR training, as well as an FBI background check. They also fulfill a certain number of hours in habilitation training, including training in medications (usually 40 hours).

It's still your responsibility, however, to interview the person the agency finds to see if his or her personality will work well with the individual needing care. Leaving a child who has no verbal skills with someone you don't really know is very difficult. The following are some criteria you might use in choosing an HTS (Habilitation Training Specialist). (1) First and foremost, pray for God to send the right person into your life. Ask for someone you can trust, as well as an individual with whom your child will feel comfortable and who will enjoy being with your child. (2) Request references from the individual, and talk to other families with whom he or she has worked. (3) Many times, God also gives that "sixth sense" that says, "This person is or is not the right one."

(4) A rule of thumb you might use is, Could I trust this person with my house, my car, and my bank account? If I handed him a thousand-dollar bill and said, "Keep this for me until I return," would he do it? If you can't answer yes to both questions, that person probably is not for you, since your child is

worth far more than any possession or amount of money.

When you finally decide on an HTS, have him or her spend time with your child while you're present in the home. Don't leave them at home alone until you're satisfied that this person is well qualified and your child is comfortable. It's not a quick process, but when you find the right person, you may be able to keep the same HTS for months or even years.

Universities sometimes have students who want to baby-sit for younger children. Many are studying to be special education teachers and welcome the chance to spend time with a child who has special needs. And don't forget to check with your church and friends. You may find a senior adult who would enjoy spending an afternoon or evening with your child. Though it's unlikely that these people will have the intensive training of an HTS, many already have CPR training. Those who don't would probably be willing to spend one Saturday morning in a class. Most hospitals provide classes regularly, and it would be wise for all parents and caregivers to have this training.

Observe Your Child

Closely observing your child to gain better understanding is one of the most important things you'll ever do for her. Learn everything about her—her ways and mannerisms. Notice what frightens, excites, or motivates her. No matter how much or how little you know about your child's disability, you need to know all the little nuances that only your child possesses.

When Jay was born, I (Louise) followed all the tips mentioned above. I read everything I could about Down syndrome. I quizzed doctors, spoke with parents, went to support-group meetings, and subscribed to such trade magazines as

Down Syndrome Congress and *Exceptional Parent*. But the best thing I did was to study Jay. I found that I would never become an expert on Down syndrome, but I could be an expert on Jay. I've learned to read his expressions, moods, and likes and dislikes, even without a lot of verbalization on his part. God has given me this ability. When I don't understand his words (not everything is on the speech device) or his desires, I pray for "divine translation."

Every child has special challenges that only you will know how to handle. One mom's advice: Never tell your child he is unable to do something, even if you feel certain he can't. You'll be shocked at how that little mind figures out a way to do it. He may not do it like other kids, but he'll do it.

Another mom advises that you not allow people to intimidate you when you're doing what you know is best for your child. Her son had a problem with tactile sensitivity and was still eating baby cereal long after well-meaning family members thought he should have been on regular food. "I was so embarrassed that I would hide the cereal under other items in the grocery cart in case I ran into someone I knew," she says. Finally, she felt so guilty about people asking when he would eat *real* cereal that she forced him to accept regular cereal for breakfast.

"Then one day I looked at that box and saw how much sugar *real* cereal has in it," says the mom. "I realized I should never have let anyone intimidate me to the point of doing something I didn't feel was in my son's best interests. I don't do that anymore. When people tell me he should be doing this or that, or that there's a better way to do something, I tell them it's not a better way because what I'm doing works!"

Remember that *you* are the authority on your child. You're the one handling the crises at home, and perhaps even at school. You get her up in the morning and listen to her prayers at night. You know all the little quirks about her—how she likes her blankets at night, what bedtime stories she enjoys, which socks don't feel right, which shirt is her favorite, and which TV programs she likes to watch. You know her learning style, her routine, how to brush her teeth, even what foods she needs to eat. Your child's teacher, therapist, and doctor don't live at your house. They don't know your child the way you do. As one dad is fond of stating, "When push comes to shove, you are the expert on your child."

I (Louise) sometimes feel as if I'm a detective on duty 24 hours a day. Yes, it's stressful at times, but look at what the alternative would be. What if I didn't really know Jay? If I didn't probe deeply enough to understand his feelings or what makes him laugh or smile, I would miss so much!

Our children are a lot like road maps with no interstate highways. Every road is "off the beaten path." Some are fun, adventurous, and full of wonderful surprises. Others are frightening and isolated. But we learn something new and valuable at each turn and junction, and then we share it with other travelers along the way. That's what makes our lives unique.

Henry David Thoreau wrote, "If a man does not keep pace with his companions, perhaps it is because he hears a different drummer. Let him step to the music which he hears, however measured or far away." Our children march to a different drummer because God has given them their own song, and it is beautiful!

Practical Gems of Wisdom

- *There is no "right" way to do things.* If everything must be customized, improvised, or tailor-made to meet

your child's needs, that's okay. This can give her the
freedom to learn and use skills in her own unique way.

- *It's essential that you become an advocate.* Learn to meet
teachers, doctors, administrators, therapists, and other
professionals eye to eye and toe to toe. Chapter 7 also
relates some practical ways to do this.

- *Not everyone will accept your child.* No matter how
much education or exposure they have, some people
simply will not accept your child. But the positive side
is that most people *will* find his innocent love
refreshing and will respond with open arms.

- *Take time for yourself.* To be an expert on your child,
you have to keep yourself healthy. Taking time off for
myself (Louise) is one of the hardest things for me to
do, because no one else knows Jay as well as I do. And
since he's home-schooled, I have sometimes taken on
the roles of mom, teacher, nurse, friend, advocate, and
even Sunday school teacher. All that can become difficult, especially if I have no relief. Not only is my
health affected, but my relationship with Jay also
suffers when I "smother" him this way. So I take small
breaks like lunch with a friend, a weekly Bible study,
and even an occasional weekend away from home
doing something I really enjoy.

- *You will never be perfect.* There will always be a parent
who seems to have things together just a little better
than you do. Comparing yourself to others is
defeating. As Wayne Hardy puts it, "It's the constant
strain of feeling guilty that you haven't done enough
for your disabled child. Jonathan has speech problems

and learning problems in addition to cerebral palsy and being in a wheelchair. He needs all sorts of therapy—physical, occupational. We need to teach him more words. There's a lack of time. Guilt can wear you down and burn you out." In the same way, there will always be another helpful conference or meeting, but you can't attend them all. Besides, we will *all* make mistakes! Learn to accept your limitations and do your best. God will honor this.

- *Learn to laugh.* When life gets too serious and responsibilities get too heavy, look for something to laugh about. There's a healing balm in laughter, and you can *always* find something humorous if you really look for it. Rent a funny video or listen to a tape of a humorous speaker. Sometimes I (Louise) just start laughing and acting silly with Jay, and suddenly everything is funny and life is lighter.

Encouragement from Scripture

- "Call unto me, and I will answer thee, and show thee great and mighty things, which thou knowest not" (Jeremiah 33:3, KJV).

- "If any of you lacks wisdom, he should ask God, who gives generously to all without finding fault, and it will be given to him" (James 1:5).

- "Being confident of this, that he who began a good work in you will carry it on to completion until the day of Christ Jesus" (Philippians 1:6).

- "In quietness and confidence is your strength" (Isaiah 30:15, TLB).

- "Trust in the LORD with all your heart and lean not on your own understanding; in all your ways acknowledge him, and he will make your paths straight" (Proverbs 3:5-6).

CHAPTER 6

BECOMING A CHAMPION: BUILDING ON YOUR CHILD'S STRENGTHS

Brian Campbell, 11 years old, stepped up to the podium at the International Carwash Association's annual convention in Las Vegas to deliver a keynote message to the 6,000 members in attendance. After rousing applause and a standing ovation, he passed out business cards—imprinted with "Professional Car Washing's #1 Fan . . . I Love Car Washes!"—and talked with the president and president-elect about new products. Circling the huge convention floor, Brian met with operators and manufacturers for hours to discuss things like the

Laserwash 4000 and a new blow-dryer called "The Stripper."

Keynoting at conventions is not a typical activity for an 11-year-old. But Brian's courage and ability to deliver a speech to a huge adult audience are even more amazing because he has a rare genetic disorder called Williams syndrome that causes heart problems, motor and coordination difficulties, and mental retardation.

Following complications at birth, Brian suffered respiratory arrest at four months, but he was given a second chance at life. When he was first diagnosed with Williams syndrome two months later, his parents, Valerie and Dale, were told to institutionalize him because he'd be severely retarded. They were also informed that they should not expect him to learn, especially in the area of reading skills. A chronically ill infant, Brian underwent open-heart surgery as well.

In spite of the negative picture painted of Brian's future, however, his parents began to read to him on his first birthday. For more than five years, they never missed a night of reading children's books to him, hoping that he would not only learn to read someday, but that he would even grow up loving books. By the age of seven, though, he still didn't know the letters of the alphabet in spite of receiving plenty of reading readiness and phonics in the special education school he attended. Trying to read books like *A Pig Can Dig* didn't interest Brian at all, and he was making no progress.

Negative into Positive

People who have Williams syndrome develop unusual obsessions, which is usually thought of as a negative characteristic. In Brian's case, his parents realized that as he overcame the fear of car washes he'd had as a preschooler, he began to be fascinated with them. They decided to capitalize on this interest, and in the process they turned what had seemed on the surface to be a negative into a positive. His favorite Saturday activity wasn't a day at the Six Flags amusement park but a family trip to a new car wash—so they had the cleanest car in the neighborhood!

His mom, Valerie, largely because of her education background and the special education courses she took after Brian's diagnosis, decided to try combining one of the strengths of the disorder, a love for language, with her son's center of learning excitement—car washes—in order to teach him to read. First she taught him several sight words with the car wash theme.

"It was almost like we worked backward by teaching him sight words first and the alphabet later," says Valerie. But it worked. She put simple words like *free, car wash, soap, enter,* and *exit* on flashcards around the house and in a word box. Immediately Brian wanted to talk about the words and their meaning. Then she would ask him to pick a word out of his word box and use it in a sentence. Next she wrote the sentence just the way he said it.

"He could always tell me what the sentence said when I asked him to read it because he had dictated it, was interested in it, and it was in *his* language," says Valerie. After he mastered the first group of words, they progressed to more-advanced words like *spot-free rinse, automatic, conveyorized belt system,* and *tunnel.*

About this time, a car wash owner in another state sent Brian an industry magazine. Now his motivation to learn to read tripled as he kept asking his mom, "What does it say under that picture? Please read me that paragraph!" The car wash magazines were his most treasured possessions. When he wanted to read the whole magazine himself, Brian was on his way to becoming a good reader.

Growing Up Learning

Now age 14 at the time of this writing, Brian can read at approximately a seventh-grade level, with fourth-grade comprehension, which continues to improve. His comprehension is much higher, however, when he deals with car wash material or something else he's interested in, like trucks or cars. This young man, whose parents were told he'd never be able to read, regularly checks out and reads books from the library. He often walks around with several books in his hand and sleeps with a pile of favorite books every night.

Since she home schools, Valerie also uses Brian's love of car washes to teach him math, a subject particularly difficult and frustrating for him. When he's working on addition facts, for example, she draws cars on a page and puts math facts on each car. From time to time, she takes him to work for a day of hands-on learning at a car wash, where the owner shows him how to run the cash register, count out change, and greet customers.

Another of Brian's strengths is using computers and calculators. Always looking for ways to help him compensate for his weaknesses, Valerie encouraged him to write most of his assignments on the computer because his poor fine-motor skills made writing by hand tedious and the results hard to read. Not only has he used the computer to E-mail letters and thank-you notes to his car-wash friends across the country, but he also enjoys creative writing. And because he excels on the computer, he learned how to use the computer control system (DRB) that operates many full-service car washes. He understands the system better than some adults do.

Hopes and Dreams

As parents, we all have hopes and dreams for our children. While a physical or mental disability can shatter our original dreams, many times God has given a compensating gift to the child. It's part of His grace. As 1 Peter 4:10 says, "God has given His grace in giving us different [or special] gifts" (authors' paraphrase).

Brian Campbell's severe heart problems, along with balance and coordination problems, keep him from being physically active. He'll never be able to ride a bike or play on a soccer team. But he's very sociable and has the confidence to walk up to a group of new people at church and carry on a conversation. He also has a network of businessmen with whom he corresponds regularly.

Here are some ways to build on your child's strengths:

- To build a child's strength in a certain area, you need to expose him to as many things as possible in his area of interest.

- Find opportunities for experience or lessons in the interest area, books to read on the topic, a magazine to subscribe to, field trips, and associations with people in that field—maybe even a mentor. With these experiences and relationships, your child can gain skills and much enjoyment.

Whose Interest?

Another important way to build on your child's strengths and help her become a champion in her own right is to look for what *she's* interested in rather than what you *want* her to be interested in. And avoid limiting your child or saying, "You can't do that because of your disability."

Louise Stewart learned this lesson from personal experience when her son Patrick asked if he could begin martial arts in the first and second grades. "He continued to insist on taking karate lessons, but in my selfishness, I tried to steer him into other activities," she says. "I was afraid he'd get hurt. I didn't think he could do it and didn't want him to be disappointed."

For a couple of years they said no to his request. But finally, it became clear to his parents that it was ridiculous to say no based on the fear that he couldn't accomplish something—for he always proved them wrong.

Patrick was born with upper bilateral femoral proximal hypoplasia—a rare birth disorder in which his thigh bones are only half as long as they should be and his hip sockets are missing. At the time he was born, only a handful of children nationwide were known to have the disorder. And in addition to having pneumonia before his first birthday, he had speech and physical therapy until age seven. Even with his disability, however, not only did he *enjoy* karate, but he also excelled quickly, more than his parents ever dreamed he could. Most children get stripes before advancing to their first belt; Patrick jumped from white belt to yellow belt in the first test. As of this writing, he's 12 years old and is close to a black belt, even though he stands only 52 inches tall.

With his karate teacher's help, Patrick learned to compensate for his weaknesses. Because of his inability to participate in most kicking exercises, for example, he substitutes for kick moves by using his strongest asset—his arms. And with one of his personality strengths—his determination—he has continued to advance. With a swift twist of his extremely strong arm,

Patrick can flip his 175-pound instructor to the floor.

Actually, Patrick doesn't think he has a physical disability; no one has ever told him he does. He may do things in a different way or use some kind of supportive equipment, but he doesn't let his disability limit his life. He takes up sports just as any other boy does. "I've treated him like our other two sons—he can do anything and accomplish anything they can. That phrase 'You can't' isn't used in our house," Louise says. "If you say, 'I can't,' you won't; but if you say, 'I'll try,' then you have a chance. I always tell our boys they have nothing to lose and everything to gain by trying—even if it's only a little."

No easy outs or excuses exist in the Stewart household! Patrick also has chores, just like his brothers. "Patrick needed some clothes washed for school, and I asked him to get up and go wash them after dinner," says his mom. "He remarked something about not being able to do it, and my 17-year-old popped back, 'What's the matter with you? You got a broken leg or something?' Patrick got up and did his laundry."

Such high expectations and encouragement have helped Patrick achieve in other areas as well. Recently, the family attended his junior high school awards assembly, where the top 10 boys out of about 400 seventh-graders were going to be honored. Since his last name started with *S,* he was in the back row of the 30 nominees on stage and couldn't be seen.

"When his name was called," Louise reports, "we could see Patrick jumping up and down and his hands waving from the back row." He was thrilled! This was an academic accomplishment, based on grades, perfect attendance, and overall attitude, that neither of his big brothers had attained. He's had many obstacles to overcome in his short life—communication and speech problems, night epilepsy, mobility—*everything* was a big challenge. But in his struggles, Patrick developed perseverance and a "Never say never" attitude.

Patrick also plays baseball and basketball and was placed first on the Disabled Swim Team of North Texas. He plays the snare drums in the school band, and his parents and school officials are trying to work out a way for him to march in the high school band. His mom and dad say they will never underestimate their son's abilities or determination again. Whatever he wants to do, they're behind him. "Being the mother of a child with a disability, all we could want is for *his* dreams to come true—not our own," she says.

Helping Your Child Learn Important Information

You can use this principle of building on strengths to teach simple, everyday, yet important things. When Jay was young, for example, I (Louise) used the 20-minute drive to his private school every morning to help him learn the names of his fellow students. Since Jay has a terrific memory and loves music, I combined the two strengths. To the tune of "Here We Go Round the Mulberry Bush," I sang, "Who are we going to see at school, see at school, see at school; Who are we going to see at school . . . early this morning?"

Jay would state a name, and we would sing, "We're going to see Michael, Michael, Michael. We're going to see Michael early this morning." Then we would start the verse again until we got through all the students, seven children in total. Not only did Jay learn every student's name, but he also had to remember whom he had already mentioned. With this music method, I never had to say, "We've already named him or her." I'd be more likely than Jay to forget!

Jay also learned about his body with songs and tunes I made up, such as, "Hey, Mister Jay, what do you say, let's sing about your body today! Say Mister Jay, where are your eyes [he would point to them] and where are your ears, just the right size [he pointed to his ears]?" We went through all the significant parts of the body this way, using music, rhyme, and silly words. One line was, "Say, Mister Jay, where's your neck so long? Now thump your chest and sing a Tarzan song." He would then beat his chest and let out a Tarzan yell.

Music has also been a way for Jay to learn many spiritual truths. He often listens to contemporary Christian music tapes. We knew he enjoyed the music but were surprised at how many deep spiritual truths he'd learned from the lyrics. Many times he has discussed a spiritual concept with us, and when asked where he learned it, he said, "The song." Then he showed us the exact tape the song was on. Jay seems to absorb spiritual truths like a sponge!

Facing Challenges with Joy

"I believe God has gifted Christine with the strengths she has to help her compensate for her visual disability," says her mother, Karen. "How imperative it is for Jack and me to help develop those strengths!" Their daughter has endured eye surgeries and many frustrations at school, but her strengths have helped her to persevere.

Besides determination, a high tolerance for pain, and strong analytical and problem-solving skills, six-year-old Christine has a delightful sense of humor and a creative, vivid imagination. Her irrepressible sense of humor and "orneryness" have been a tremendous boost to their family. "Without her, things would be very serious and dull around our house," Karen says. Christine has taught her parents and sister to laugh, play tricks on each other, and not take life so seriously. In response, they've loosened their collars and encouraged the laughter through squirt guns, ice cubes down the back, word play, and silly jokes told in the car while traveling.

Christine has a whole host of imaginary friends; her dolls all have names and ages that Mommy is supposed to remember. Christine often has a half-hour conversation with her dolls as she dreams up imaginary plays and characters. The family's nickname for her is Tigger because, like the A. A. Milne character, she bounces wherever she goes. Her kindergarten teacher is helping her write her stories down. And who knows, with the encouragement of her parents and teachers, where this gift of creativity will lead her in adulthood?

Knowing the challenges her daughter will face in a town dominated by competitive team sports, Karen also has Christine in individual pursuits like piano, gymnastics, and swimming. She will continue looking for and developing her daughter's gifts as they emerge. Sometimes a talent surprises them, as Karen relates in the story below:

> One Sunday, while we were getting ready for church, Christine wanted to sing a song she'd made up. "Not now," I told her. When we arrived at church, she asked again. I said yes but only half listened as I laid music on the children's chairs for primary opening exercises.
>
> She finished and asked, "Can I sing that for Sunday school?"
>
> I tried to explain that it wouldn't be fair to the other children, that we all sang together during Sunday school.
>
> "Can I sing it for church?"
>
> Impatient, I said, "Christine, the program is already set. You have to ask the people who plan the worship service, and they schedule the special music." It was a shaky expla-

nation that I didn't think she understood but the best I could do at the moment.

"Who does the program?" this six-year-old persisted.

I told her, then turned back to my task, unaware that she had left.

Soon she was back at my side. "Bonnie said I could sing my song after the children's sermon," she announced proudly.

Now she had my full attention. I made a beeline for Bonnie. "Do you know what this child is doing?" I sputtered.

"Yes, isn't it wonderful?" she coolly replied.

"Bonnie, she just made it up. You have no idea what she's going to get up there and do," I told her.

But Bonnie wouldn't budge either. "It's great she's so willing. 'Except that we become like little children . . .'" she quoted as she bustled off.

I worried all through the Sunday school hour and asked my friend Betty to start praying. My preacher husband came to sit beside me during the children's sermon. I whispered to him what was about to happen. He flinched visibly and looked at his watch. "We're running short on time as it is," he groaned.

"I know, I know," I soothed. "But something tells me we just need to trust. Besides, the scripture keeps coming to me, 'If anyone has a song . . .'"

"Even your six-year-old daughter," he said with a grimace.

The children's sermon was over. I stood up. Perhaps I needed to sit in the front pew to show her where to stand (*After all, she can't see where she's going*, I reasoned) and to prompt her in case of a disaster. But Bonnie had beat me to it and was already situating Christine in front of the mike. Something—or Someone—said inside me, "Sit down; let her go." I slumped in the pew but then perched on the edge, full of anxiety.

Christine, however, was cool. "I'm going to sing you a song," she told the congregation. "It doesn't have a title because I made it up. It has four verses."

And she proceeded to sing a lovely song: "Thank You for the world so sweet . . . God, You made it good." By the third verse, tears were streaming down my face.

"How was my sermon this morning?" my husband asked after the service.

"I don't know," I honestly replied. "I didn't hear the first half of it because I was still bawling." Another verse had come to my mind: "And a little child shall lead them." We had been so intent on sticking to the schedule that we had almost missed God's moving in the heart of a little child. He used the simplicity and confidence of my own daughter to make my heart open to His leading once again.

"How do you think God felt when you sang your song, Christine?" I asked her later.

She cocked her head. "Happy," she said with a smile, and then she went back to her book.

I'm sure He was.

Looking for Gifts

Look for your child's strengths, for the compensating gifts God gives: an incredible smile that melts the hardest heart; a gift of compassion; musical ability; the desire and ability to pray for others. Applying the suggestions below will help increase your awareness.

- Observe how your child plays and what interests him the most.

- Watch how she interacts with others—siblings, classmates, teachers, and therapists. She may do things at school that she doesn't do for you at home.

- How does he learn things best? How does he compensate? For example, if he learns best by *hearing* information, you can get an audio tape of a book he's assigned for school. (These are provided free for both visually impaired people and those with language or learning disabilities.) If he has good music memory and aptitude, show him how to set information he needs to learn to music, as the story above about Jay demonstrates.

- What does your child respond to, and how can you integrate this into her daily lifestyle? If it's art, for example, how could you use art to enrich her life? You might provide opportunities for drawing and painting to stimulate her creativity (for children with developmental disabilities, creativity may not come naturally but will need stimulation). Drawing or painting a picture could also help her work through a loss, such as the death of a grandparent, or express her feelings about a difficult hospital experience.

- Avoid pushing your child into the mold of what the rest of the family excels at or is interested in. Accept him as he is; let him be himself and have his own interests and skills.

- Avoid focusing so much on your child's weaknesses that you hinder your ability to identify her strengths. For example, a common characteristic of ADD children is the often sensitized ability to nurture and enjoy younger children. ADD kids often appear in the neighborhood as "mother ducks" with a train of ducklings trailing behind. The reason? In a word, ADD children are *fun*. They know how to utilize their imaginations to create innovative games and activities. Embracing this positive characteristic by providing opportunities within the family can help give them a much-needed sense of belonging.

- Pray for eyes to see the uniqueness of your child and his special, God-given gift. Look for that gift; pray for God to reveal it to you. Then encourage your child in that area. Develop a bigger view of gifting; include spiritual gifts like a servant's heart, intercession, mercy, and so on. God's Word tells us the greatest of all the gifts is *love*.

One Valentine's Day, the Shanafelt family was taking time after dinner to encourage one another. When it came to Jason's turn, he ran upstairs and brought down all the candy he'd received that day at school. Then he went around the room, giving each family member a big hug, saying "I love you," and handing out some candy. He ended up giving away all the candy, saving none for himself. His love and care for his siblings and parents continues to touch their lives every day.

Challenged Children: Facing Difficulties and Making Progress

Challenged children often face huge difficulties but are tremendous blessings. "My son's openness is one of his gifts, and he has taught us invaluable lessons about what really matters in life," says Wayne Hardy. Recently he asked his son Jonathan, age seven, who has cerebral palsy, "Jonathan, what am I going to do with you?"

"Love me," he said.

Kyle is a 17-year-old who faced many obstacles in early childhood. He had language problems, learning disabilities, and ADHD (attention deficit with hyperactivity disorder). He zoomed around a room and couldn't sit still. His gross motor skills were deficient. His first preschool teacher told his mom she saw signs of autism, and because of aggressive behavior he was asked to leave.

But Georgia, his mom, continued to believe that God had given Kyle a gift, and she was determined to find it. And finally she did. Kyle hadn't been good in swimming when she enrolled him in lessons as a nine-year-old, but two years later, his teacher in a learn-to-swim class called his mother and told her he had lots of potential as a swimmer. The teacher convinced Kyle to join the swim club, and he got better and better and started winning races. Recently, Kyle became the Pennsylvania state champion, winning the gold medal in the 100-yard butterfly and silver in the 500-yard freestyle. He also took fifth place at junior nationals.

Swimming also helped Kyle develop other skills, like self-control and discipline, that have paid off in the classroom. He's now on the Distinguished Honor Roll at school because of his hard work. He still has problems sometimes with organization, however. He gets frustrated with some academic tasks, but the medication Ritalin has helped his concentration and focus.

For a little boy who got expelled from preschool, Kyle has come a long way. His picture hangs outside his high school gym as an all-state swimmer, and he has been accepted at a good prep school for his junior and senior years.

"Swimming is a gift in so many ways for Kyle," says Georgia. "If each mother could look for God's gift in her child, no matter what his problems or disabilities, and nurture it, what amazing things she might discover!"

Overcoming Obstacles to Achieve

My (Cheri's) niece Eve was diagnosed with juvenile rheumatoid arthritis in early adolescence. Born with a hole in her heart, she had open heart surgery at five and has suffered with asthma throughout her life. Although unable to participate in athletics through junior high and high school, Eve worked hard in the classroom. She kept up with her work even through several rounds of chemotherapy in high school and two hand and wrist surgeries in her senior year, finishing at the top of her class.

When the Ponder High School graduation ceremonies arrived, I watched as Eve got up from her chair time after time to receive first one award and then another and another—a total of 12 in all. She was salutatorian of her class, and she also won a National Honor Society Merit Award, the top awards in chemistry, physics, and math, a Christian leadership scholarship from Dallas Baptist University, where she would attend college, and others. Her goal is to work in the field of medicine with children someday.

Becoming a Champion

During the summer Olympics in 1976, Bonnie Shepherd was in the hospital delivering a nine-and-a-half-pound son, Adam. Her husband held the baby up as all the Olympic athletes were marching by on the TV screen and said, "Here is *our* champ!" Although his name was Adam, they often called him "Champ."

However, when it became obvious that their little champ was not as physically able as he should be—when Adam wasn't hitting the milestones such as rolling over or sitting up as other babies his age were—"little champion" took on another meaning.

"It was a word that almost mocked us for a while," says Bonnie. "Yet he really was a champ, because we saw how he struggled to roll over, struggled to get up on his knees to crawl." Adam *was* a champion, scooting on his back and heels for two and a half years, determined to be mobile.

The first time he held onto a

Recently a sports reporter interviewed my now 20-year-old son, Justin, about his place on the U. S. tennis team for the Special Olympics World Games. As I watched their interchange, I was amazed at Justin's poised and well-thought-out answers to the reporter's questions. So what if he can read only at a first- or second-grade level—he sure can talk!

I was a little taken aback when the reporter asked me, "Was it hard when Justin was growing up?"

Was it hard? My thoughts returned to the early days when Justin was so frustrated, so hyperactive, so competitive, so needy. "Yes, it was hard," I admitted. "But his father and I believed then, as we do now, that all children need the same things—unconditional love, encouragement, challenge, and accountability. It's just that children with special challenges such as Justin's need everything with an extra dose of patience, love, and grace."

— Lucinda Secrest McDowell

walker was at a roller rink with his friends from school. They turned on the lights of the roller rink and let Adam go out on the big floor with his walker, and he walked all over the place, pushing it around. The kids cheered. Another victory had happened.

Adam rose to so many challenges through the years. And when his parents watched their son participate in the Special Olympics, those words came back to them—words they'd heard during the summer Olympics the year of their son's birth.

When Adam came across that goal line, winning his first gold medal in Special Olympics, they thought, *Yep, we do have a champion!*

Sometimes God gives you things in ways different from what you think. It was no less a moment of pride for Adam or us than if he were winning an Olympic gold medal. You realize that life is full of little milestones along the way. When you're told your special child can't do many things, you can look at all those things, or you can look at what he is doing.

Focus on those accomplishments. I got so tired of hearing "These kids can't," and I've kind of carried a slogan around for years that said, "Our kids can!"

—*Bonnie Shepherd*

An Extraordinary Life

We love what Judy Squier, a radiant Christian who was born with no legs, wrote to the family of a little boy born without arms and legs:

The first thing I would say is that all that this entails is at least one hundred times harder on the parents than the child. A birth defect by God's grace does not rob childhood of its wonder, nor is a child burdened by high expectations. Given a supportive, creative, and loving family, I know personally that I enjoyed not a less-than-average life nor an average life, but as I've told many, my life has been not ordinary but extraordinary. I am convinced without a doubt that a loving heavenly Father oversees the creative miracles in the inner sanctum of each mother's womb (Psalm 139), and that in His sovereignty there are no accidents.

What the caterpillar calls the end of the world, the Creator calls a butterfly. As humanity we see only the imperfect underside of God's tapestry of our lives. What we judge to be "tragic—the most dreaded thing that could happen," I expect we'll one day see as the awesome reason for the beauty and uniqueness of our life and our family. (*Adapted from "There Are No Accidents" in Elisabeth Elliot's* Keep a Quiet Heart *[Ann Arbor, Mich.: Servant, 1995], pp. 29-30.*)

Encouragement from Scripture

- "God has given each of you some special abilities; be sure to use them to help each other, passing on to others God's many kinds of blessings" (1 Peter 4:10, TLB).

- "Guard well the splendid, God-given ability you received as a gift from the Holy Spirit who lives within you" (2 Timothy 1:14, TLB).

- "I can do everything through him who gives me strength" (Philippians 4:13).

- "Finally, be strong in the Lord and in his mighty power" (Ephesians 6:10).

- "God has given each of us the ability to do certain things well" (Romans 12:6, TLB).

- "He who began a good work in you will carry it on to completion until the day of Christ Jesus" (Philippians 1:6).

CHAPTER 7

BECOMING YOUR CHILD'S ADVOCATE

At the end of elementary school, Chris Jones's parents faced a decision. Should they keep him in the county deaf education program in a school across the county or move him to be the first and only hearing-impaired child mainstreamed at Ramblewood Middle School, the neighborhood school his brother attended? A serious case of spinal meningitis at 11 months of age had caused hearing loss, and Chris was diagnosed as severely to profoundly deaf. His parents felt that after speech therapy in his preschool years, tutoring with an oral teacher in her home, and learning sign language in his elementary years, he was ready for the challenge of their neighborhood school.

Chris already communicated well with kids in the neighborhood, on his hockey team, and at church. Dottie, his mom, reports that as she prayed with a friend about what God's best would be for Chris, "Before I got the 'Amen' on the prayer, I knew we were to have him mainstreamed at the middle school with an interpreter." She felt the deaf education program was a "feel good" program with weaker academics than Chris needed. Yet she knew her son would face big challenges in the regular school. She and her husband talked to Chris about the decision and the obstacles he'd face, and he was enthusiastic about it. So his mom called a meeting before school started.

At that meeting, Chris's private speech pathologist documented how they would continue to take care of his speech therapy needs. In addition, a child advocate that Dottie had brought along underscored the benefits for Chris. Nonetheless, the school personnel were strongly *against* moving Chris out of the deaf education program. Dottie faced big opposition, because the school district had never had a profoundly deaf child at the middle school. Even after Dottie carefully explained her reasons, they said, "We can't understand why you'd want to do this, and it's not our recommendation." They saw only the risks and potential problems.

After much discussion, a compromise was reached. Chris could go to the middle school for sixth grade but would have to start out in the ESE (Exceptional Student Education) class, with mainstreaming only in math and social studies. His interpreter, provided by the school district, turned out to be a former missionary who became a special friend of the family. And Chris did so well that after the first semester, the school allowed him to take additional regular classes.

The next year, Chris was fully mainstreamed, and he has maintained A's, B's, and C's in all his classes in the community high school. An outgoing self-starter at 16, he has many friends and excels at roller hockey. Since he has his driver's license now, he drives himself to speech therapy after school. His parents have no doubt that their decision to move him in sixth grade was the right thing for their son, although it took planning, persistence, and compromise in the beginning.

The Importance of Information and Professionalism

Like Dottie, if you're the parent of a special-needs child, you need to become an effective advocate for your child. So many decisions have to be made that affect your child's development: choosing the best school programs, finding the least-restrictive environment, locating agencies that can assist you. There's so much to learn! How can you be the best possible advocate for your child?

Step one is to arm yourself with information. Find out what services are available to assist parents, what the laws say, and how to interpret those laws. The best way to begin the process is

When we see our children suffer from a disability that seems to affect every facet of their lives, our hearts may prompt us to find ways to minimize their struggle by doing all we can to fix their broken lives.

While we need to consistently communicate our willingness to come alongside them in their struggles, we must not rob them of an even greater gift—teaching and allowing them to advocate for themselves, especially in areas where they're able.

Watching one of my sons with ADD struggle in school this year has tempted me, over and over, to intervene beyond what would be helpful. Desiring more to equip than to handicap him, I found myself expressing to him my concern for his struggles, reminding him of my commitment to stand with him, yet pressing him to accept these problems and challenges as his own. I've learned that guiding Dave in problem-solving techniques increases his belief that he is able to successfully negotiate the options.

— Kathy Vugteveen

to attend parent training. "Every state has a PTI, or Parent Training and Information Center, funded under the IDEA (Individuals with Disabilities Education Act)," says Dara Howe, a parent advocate for the Tennessee Disability Coalition and the mother of a child with special needs. In their state, for example, parents can get advocate training at the STEP Center (Support and Training for Exceptional Parents).

One resource for finding out where the parent training is in your state and community is the annual January issue of *Exceptional Parent* magazine. You can also call the special education department of your local school district or one of the local advocacy organizations like Easter Seals or United Cerebral Palsy and ask them who has the grant for parent training in your state.

Step two is to learn how to behave as a professional in all your discussions with educators and administrators who interact with your child. If you're perceived as a professional, you'll be treated with more respect. See yourself as an equal to those who run programs that serve your child, and never refer to yourself as "just a parent." You are the most important person in your child's life. When you sit at a meeting, you know more about your child than anyone else.

"The way to get over feeling intimidated by professionals," says Dara, "is to gain knowledge and information and realize how important your understanding of your child is."

Debbie Jeffers had found signing beneficial with her daughter Ashlee, who has a hearing deficit in one ear. But the school district (which had labeled her as mentally retarded) refused to acknowledge Ashlee as hearing impaired and thus would provide neither signing in her classroom nor a special program.

After Debbie taught Ashlee's teacher some basic sign language, the teacher began working with a deaf-education instructor to learn the core words that she would use in her curriculum each week. She then taught Ashlee those key words by signing, which significantly increased her vocabulary and comprehension. A few months later, before a scheduled IEP (individualized education plan) meeting, Debbie called several organizations and found one that would send an educational advocate with her to the meeting. That's all it took. The school agreed to the curriculum and the changes Debbie requested.

Being an advocate means knowing your child and his needs and having a vision of his future. You need to know where he's going and never underestimate his potential. If given the opportunity, resources, and educational environment that's right for him, he may well amaze you with what he can do.

Building Relationships

Whether you're going into an IEP, ARD (admission, review,

Moms, Oatmeal, and School Buses

For years, Jan's breakfast was the hardest meal of the day for her to eat. Because of morning congestion, she would choke and spit, sputter and cough with almost every spoonful. One day, I had an early appointment. I put on my makeup and clothes and then put on a robe to protect my clothing. I hurriedly fed Jan, and we waited for her school bus to arrive. As soon as she was safely on board, I pulled off my robe, stepped into my shoes, and raced out the door to my car. As I backed my car out of the garage, I took a quick look at the rearview mirror and saw that my carefully styled and sprayed hair had a big, gooey glob of oatmeal right on top of it. I kept thinking the rest of the day, Thank You, God, that I looked in that mirror!

—*Pam Whitley*

and dismissal), or M (multidisciplinary) Team meeting, personal relationships are a key part of getting full implementation. There's a difference between what a piece of paper says about rights and how the child is actually treated. For many children who have tremendous needs in different areas, you can't ever rest; there's always something else to work on to get their needs met. So you have to pace yourself, set your goals, and pick your battles. Prioritize the most important things, and work on one at a time. When you see all the needs, it's easy to be overwhelmed. Think, *What does my child need the most right now?* and work on that.

Instead of entering into meetings with a confrontational attitude, begin on a friendly basis. Don't go in expecting problems or assuming the worst, even if you've heard a bad report from another parent.

Dara Howe advises using a strategy of kindness. "If I'm going to be asking for something different for my child, I do all I can to soften up those making decisions," she says. "I start the meeting with pleasant chitchat and pass compliments around instead of focusing on what the professionals aren't doing for my child. I even make cookies and do things that I normally do for people I like. If we behave in a way that's kind, people want to help us. So smile a lot and be positive and lavish with your praise. Softening the edges and using your best interpersonal skills pays off. That's part of being an advocate and an ambassador for your child. Being an advocate doesn't mean bullying, demanding, or dictating what people have to do."

Setting Goals

Judy Meine, mother of four children, including Natalie, 11, who has severe cerebral palsy, feels a key to success with school officials is keeping an open mind and being willing to compromise. "There are all kinds of things I said I'd never do: I wanted her in full inclusion; I didn't want her in special education. But this year I agreed to it, because the teacher is a specialist in augmentative communication, which Natalie needs. Before, when she was in a special education room, it was more like baby-sitting than productive learning time."

Judy sits down with her husband, Michael, and discusses the goals for Natalie's education that year, and they both have input in writing her IEP. She takes the curriculum for Natalie's grade level and picks out the items that can be adapted for her. Then Judy meets with the teacher before the IEP meeting, and they integrate their family's goals with the teacher's. "I make sure the IEP is totally fitted to Natalie's needs," Judy says. "They once gave her a computer-generated, standardized IEP and checked off goals. I asked that it be thrown out and an original plan created. We began to see progress from that."

Then at the meeting, Judy and the teacher walk in with a united vision for Natalie and are clearly working together. "My goal as a parent is to support the teacher and facilitate Natalie's learning rather than work against the teacher," Judy says. "I try to get the teacher the help she needs. If I don't ask for that help in the meeting, like extra training or equipment she needs for Natalie, it may not be available." They don't always get everything they request, but that's where compromise comes in.

Judy is also the PTA representative for the special education children and their parents, and the room-parent coordinator for the whole school. This involvement has really paid off. As a member of the PTA board, she has built relationships and gotten to know the administrators and other parents. Since Natalie's third grade teacher is the teachers' representative on the PTA board, they see each other for that extra time each month, allowing the teacher to know Judy in a different way than just as Natalie's mom. The principal, too, has been willing to try different things for Natalie because he knows teachers will get the support they need from Judy.

In the first few weeks of a new school year, Judy lets the teachers get to know Natalie and become more comfortable with her. Then she starts checking with them by phone or stopping in to see if there are some supplies she could send to help out or equipment the family has at home that would be useful at school. She has sent adapted games Natalie uses at home that can benefit the whole class, and she has looked at discount stores and garage sales for art and craft supplies and other materials to give to the teacher.

Building Communication

Being a teacher herself, Sandy Warren knows how vital it is to get to know her daughter Jan's teacher and communicate regularly. Then if she has a question about something, she doesn't mind asking it, and the teacher makes recommendations more freely. "I make friends with the people who deal with my daughter," says Sandy. Knowing special education classrooms always need something, she asks what the teacher needs that she could buy or make. She buys the teacher a present for Christmas and at the end of the year to show her appreciation. She has found that even a computer mouse or a package of new construction paper is appreciated. A parent with limited finances could cut out letters for the bulletin board or make something the class needs.

Since communication is important and her daughter is non-verbal, Sandy has found that a spiral notebook is a great way to keep in touch with Jan's teacher. The notebook goes in Jan's book bag and travels back and forth between home and school.

Sandy writes a note every morning to the teacher with information such as that Jan was up until 4:00 that morning; that Jan has been sick and is on antibiotics; or that when Jan signs *airplane,* she's referring to the fact that in two months her college-student brothers are coming home, and the family will pick them up at the airport. Then the teacher writes back to Sandy each day about problems, good things, progress Jan made at school, questions, and whatever information Sandy needs to know.

"That everyday dialogue has made a world of difference in how we can do things," Sandy says. "It brings a continuity between home and school. It lessens Jan's anxiety and frustration. And especially if you have a child who is not verbal, you miss out on all that communication over milk and cookies. The daily notebook dialogue works even if you're at a full-time job and not able to be at the school."

Before the IEP

Here are some ways to prepare before meeting with educators and professionals to develop your child's individualized education plan:

1. Determine what your child has accomplished since his last IEP. Review records and notes on past meetings. Collect records you will need to share. What was your main goal? Has it been accomplished? Is it still relevant?

2. Look at your child's life now—what is she doing? What does she need? Does she actually need occupational therapy, or is it a hassle for 30 minutes a week? What skills would you most like your child to learn? What do you believe are her strengths and weaknesses? Focus on the big things—the main goals you want to reach and how to achieve them. Are new materials needed? Would a different approach help?

3. Write down a list of questions you want to ask, information you'd like the teacher to be aware of, and suggestions you have for your child's program.

4. Visit with the teacher before the conference, and get her input. What does *she* think your child's strengths and weaknesses are right now? Where has she seen improvement? Where is he lacking? What would help her facilitate the goals you've set for your child?

5. With the teacher's feedback and your goals, determine what you want to bring to the IEP meeting, and propose how it can be accomplished. For example, if your child needs to work more on math, you could suggest a computer program that makes it fun. Come up with different options.

6. Be on time to the IEP meeting. Take your spouse and/or a friend who is an educator, even an outside professional if needed. Since objectives are often worded in an unusual or technical way, read everything carefully when the IEP is finished. Check to see if there are starting and ending times for goals.

You can even take the IEP home and study it if you don't feel comfortable signing it at the meeting.

7. Remember that you, the parent, are the expert on your child. That expertise isn't based on what degree you have; you simply know your child best. Be gracious. Give in where it doesn't matter, but fight for the big things that will make a difference in your child's life and learning.

8. After the meeting, *before* signing the IEP, check your notes. Make sure that all goals are covered and you and the school personnel are in agreement. Then discuss the plan with your spouse and child if they weren't present.

Don't Burn Your Bridges

Sometimes parents get irritated by how their child is treated, what professionals say in a meeting, or what is lacking in services. "But no matter how frustrated you are, don't say anything to a professional you wouldn't want them to say to you," says Dara Howe. "If you want to maintain a good relationship, keep a civil tongue and behave professionally. You never know when you might have to come back and ask that person for something your child really needs."

Although the IEP is supposed to include a discussion of the child's strengths, it's not uncommon for school personnel to focus only on deficits. Always go back to these questions: What progress has my child made? What does he need in order to reach his potential in some area?

Almost every parent of a child with special needs has been

given a negative report in some area or told that the child will never do something. Instead of being flattened by such a report, have a realistic vision of your child and her future, but don't allow the school to discount the possibilities of what she could do, especially if her disabilities are physical or technology might prove helpful. Recent technologies have opened many new doors for children with handicaps. For example, with voice-output computers, people with very limited abilities can communicate and manipulate their environment. The possibilities will increase even more in the future, so keep up with developments in technology that would help your child, and keep the team informed.

The Mainstreaming/Inclusion Issue

One of the important decisions parents of children with disabilities face—and in which they may need to be a strong advocate for their kids—is whether their child should be in a self-contained special education classroom or mainstreamed. Although all parents must decide this based on what their child's special needs are, it helps to look at the pros and cons of mainstreaming and inclusion and the key considerations to keep in mind when choosing.

Mainstreaming means having a special education student in the regular classroom part of the school day (which could be 30 minutes or several class periods), whereas *inclusion* means the child is fully included in all regular classes for the entire school day, generally with an aide or special education teacher providing the help and resources the child needs to function well.

Inclusion is the goal of many parents because, as one mom said, "We can't have a child educated in self-contained special ed classrooms and only included in art or music and then graduate and know how to function in normal society." In addition, one of the problems with just a token mainstreaming situation is that then the child is only a visitor in the class-room. The other students don't feel that the child is part of the class. With inclusion, you provide a lot of special resources—an aide and so on—especially at the beginning of the year. As the year progresses, the classmates begin to take on part of the child's support, such as pushing the wheelchair from class to class and helping the child in the lunchroom or on the play-ground.

Inclusion has its own challenges, however. It can be difficult, depending on the degree of disability, to include a child in all aspects of the school day. Further, many general education teachers resist having disabled children in their classrooms because they feel they aren't provided enough special resources to meet their needs, and they may already be overburdened. In good programs, the special education teacher goes into the reg-ular classroom as a resource to both the teacher and the dis-abled student, or else an aide is provided.

Let's look more closely at the pros and cons of having a spe-cial-needs child included in the regular classroom for part or all of the school day:

PROS

Good role modeling: Natalie is in the honors reading group in her class. The teacher put her there because when the top read-ers read aloud, it's good reinforcement for her, and Natalie benefits enormously from the interaction with her classmates. The students love having Natalie in their group and fight over who gets to sit by her and help her.

Boost to self-esteem: If the resources are provided so the special-needs child can experience success and learn effectively, it's a great boost to his self-image. Being included also helps the child feel like a regular kid.

Socialization: Peer interaction and relationships can form between the disabled child and the other students that are valuable and a blessing for both. Participating in cooperative groups on projects means students, both special ed and regular ed, can work together and learn from each other.

Challenge for the child: The regular classroom has activities that can be challenging and stimulating to the special-needs child. Creativity can be encouraged through art activities and other creative projects, which is important for all children.

CONS

Lack of one-on-one help: The disabled child may not get the one-on-one assistance she needs to function well and be successful; she may need more direction or help than can be provided in the regular classroom, in which case the parent may have to provide extra tutoring or other support after school.

Inability to participate fully: The special-needs child may not be able to perform at grade level and therefore might not be able to participate in some activities or assignments. Whether he can participate fully has a lot to do with whether an aide, other support, and/or modifications of assignments are provided, which the special education teacher is supposed to handle.

Absence of "safe" surroundings: The child isn't in the protected environment of the special ed classroom. Accidents happen, and there may be an occasional negative remark or mean child. Karen's third-grade classmates were pushing her in her wheelchair on the playground one day when it turned over, scraping her arm. Karen's mom didn't get upset or pull her out of the regular classroom, however, because she has decided that normal kids have little accidents, too, and she feels the benefits of the good relationships and activities Karen enjoys there are worth an occasional problem.

Inclusion Versus the Special Ed Classroom: Key Considerations

In deciding between inclusion and the special education classroom, parents must figure out where their comfort zone is and what risks they are willing to take with their child. This includes facing their fears, since placing the child in the regular class—out of the protection of the special ed classroom—can be scary for parent and student. (Usually, however, parents have more worries in this area.)

How much are the parents willing to be involved—to help the teacher come up with adaptations and modifications, to support the teacher and the school? In the IEP meeting at the first of the year, it's wise to make sure all the supports and resources are in place for the teacher so the special-needs child is not a burden or a problem in the classroom.

For example, if your child needs an aide's help to participate in art activities, be sure that's provided. If your child is profoundly hearing impaired, an aide/interpreter who can assist in language activities would be vital. Checking regularly with the classroom teacher throughout the year is important, too.

Weigh the pros and cons and see what's best for your child. What are your goals for him, and can they best be met in the special ed classroom, the regular ed classroom, or a combination of the two?

If the principal is inclusion-minded and provides the support the teacher needs, that's a big plus. On the other hand, regardless of what the child's IEP says, if the principal is against inclusion, there may well be problems.

Likewise, if the regular classroom teacher your child is assigned to is positive about her being a part of the class, it will be a much more positive learning experience than otherwise.

Sometimes compromise is necessary; rarely do parents get everything they want for their child. James, a third-grader who has cerebral palsy, is in general ed three hours a day and in the special ed classroom four hours a day. He needs physical and speech therapy, which are provided in the special ed classroom. He's still in diapers, and the regular classroom teacher can't take care of those needs, either. Some kids are medically fragile or have such severe behavior problems that it's difficult to meet their needs in the regular classroom. *Always go back to your goals for your child and where and how they can best be met.*

Due Process

The standard way of handling a need for services or a problem is through the IEP meeting and/or the director of special services or special education. Most schools will do everything possible to mediate with parents in order to avoid a due process hearing, which is both time-consuming and costly to the school. However, if a parent has a grievance that is not resolved in the child's best interests, the parent can choose to file a due process suit against the school. In the same way, if the parent refuses to cooperate with school officials in a way that they believe is necessary for the child's best interests, they can file a due process suit against the parent.

One family, for example, requested a home-based teacher for

their daughter because her immune system was so deficient that she had suffered 13 upper-respiratory infections the previous year, some causing medical complications, and she had only been exposed to a small group of children. The school, however, refused the request.

When the parents appealed, explaining in detail why this teaching situation was needed, the district special services director said a doctor's recommendation would be needed. The child's doctor wrote such a letter, but at the IEP meeting, the director decided that the letter didn't state what the state board of education required. So the doctor wrote two more letters confirming the medical reasons for the child to receive home-based teaching services. After the fifth meeting and several attempts at mediation through the Protection and Advocacy Center (which provides free legal services to parents of special-needs children), the parents filed a due process suit.

The school district again refused to mediate and got extensions that lasted almost a year, but the actual hearing brought a positive outcome for the child. She has been schooled at home ever since, which resulted in fewer infections and much better health, and she has made significant progress with her teacher and parents working together.

Every state has a policies and procedures manual for special education that explains parents' rights in education, IEPs, placement, least-restrictive environment, and so on. Any question you might have should be covered in the manual, as well as the laws that exist to ensure that all eligible children with disabilities have available to them a free, appropriate public education as mandated by the Individuals with Disabilities Education Act (IDEA). Free to any parent who requests one from the state department of education, the manual includes complaint procedures, the current laws, a list of your state's special education

Seven Things Disabled Kids Want You to Know

1. ACCEPT ME FOR WHO I AM.
Don't be afraid to get to know me. I may be slow physically or mentally, but I'm good company when you give me a chance. Take time to enjoy me. I like being invited to go places and do things with friends, but I don't get invited very often.

2. SOMETIMES I NEED A FRIEND.
I need a friend who can help me break down the barriers that isolate me from the rest of the world. I can't get places without help. For instance, when I have trouble reading, you could sit by me and read the lesson in Sunday school or sing the hymn in church service so I can hear the words.

3. TALK TO ME AS YOU WOULD TO ANY OTHER PERSON.
Don't speak to me in baby talk. I'm not an infant or a pet. At times, I may have difficulty and my speech may sound different, but I try to say the words right. Sometimes I talk by signing with my hands. When you talk, just slow down a bit.

4. LET ME TRY TO DO MY BEST.
I may take longer and need your patience, but I might surprise you

administrators, and special-services workers in your state and city. Be sure to ask for the most up-to-date edition.

In addition to a section on writing an IEP, the manual includes pages of resources for parents, such as the Disability Law Center, Legal Aid, and other helpful organizations. The manual also explains the steps involved in the due process hearing if you have to take that route.

Educating Others About Your Child

Advocacy also means educating others about your child, whether that's teaching empathy in the classroom or helping those who work with your child to see her as an individual.

"I always try to help her teachers and classmates see Natalie as part of a family and not just as a handicapped child," says Judy Meine. At the class's family picnic, for example, she took Natalie's teenage brother and little brothers, Clint and Matthew, so everyone could see Natalie as the big sister. Clint ran around, playing with her wheelchair and interacting with his sister. Judy wanted everyone to see that Natalie is one of four kids and is *not* the center of attention at home.

"The point I try to get across to her teachers and classmates is that Natalie is a child with a disability—the disability is not Natalie," says her mom. "She has a personality, her own opinions, and things she delights in—she just has a harder time expressing herself since she's nonverbal." One way Judy has done this was to make a photo album of Natalie's summer experiences at Camp Easter Seals and send it to school. She got to show it to the teacher and her classmates. They couldn't believe Natalie had gone up the 50-foot-high wall of the obstacle course and went across the zip line. They were amazed at all she did at camp and loved the photos. Judy also sent another album of Natalie—when she was born, how she grew, her

with what I can do. Don't do things for me. Ask me if I want help. I'm proud of my work, even if it isn't perfect. And please, don't go back and redo it.

5. DON'T FEEL SORRY FOR ME. *I enjoy life and can make yours a little brighter, but only if you let me. If we respect each other, we can learn from each other.*

6. BE PATIENT WHEN I MESS UP. *I sometimes say and do things that aren't appropriate. By carefully explaining things to me, you can help me learn proper social skills. Be understanding when things don't go well.*

7. KNOW THAT I LOVE GOD—AND HE LOVES ME. *I know the Lord doesn't love me more than others, but I also know He keeps me close to His heart. God placed me on earth for a reason. He knows all my imperfections, and best of all, He loves me just the way I am. Can you do the same? (Anita Corrine Donihue, Focus on the Family, August 1996.)*

family, when she was in early childhood and kindergarten at other schools, and even her trip to New England to see her grandmother and aunt.

Teaching Empathy and Overcoming Barriers

Dani Steiger found a creative way to tell the kids in her son's third-grade room that classmates who are different in some ways have feelings the same as theirs. Having fragile X syndrome means Daniel is easily distracted, has autistic tendencies, and is sensitive to noises and crowds. But like the other boys and girls in his class, he likes to swim, have friends, go to Disneyland, and watch movies. When Daniel moved from his small special ed classroom to be mainstreamed in regular classes a few hours a day, his mother wanted the other kids to understand why Daniel does certain things and to know ways to be his friend.

To that end, she made a video to show his class of Daniel swimming, diving, climbing into his grandpa's treehouse, and blowing out birthday candles. She wanted his classmates to know the meaning of empathy.

"How many of you ride a bike?" she asked in the presentation. "What would you do if there were no brakes? Well, Daniel's brain doesn't have brakes."

Next she asked, "How many of you have felt frustrated, misunderstood, picked on, or scared? Daniel feels like that every day."

She went on to explain some of Daniel's specific difficulties. She told the children that if they wanted to be Daniel's friend, they could ask him to play, and if he said no, they could ask him to watch them play. They could also talk to him about any children's movie—he's sure to have seen it—and about sharks or musical instruments.

Dani ended by saying, "Daniel can't do everything you can do, but he can feel everything you can feel. Daniel didn't choose to be the way he is, but you can choose—to help him or to hurt him."

The 20-minute video and presentation were so effective that teachers asked Dani to offer it in 11 classrooms, with all the students who share Daniel's schedule. They found that her message that everyone is different and has strengths and weaknesses applies universally.

The presentation helped children relate to Daniel and become more accepting, encouraging, and even protective of him. By sharing his journey of confusion and difficulty, courage and perseverance, classmates were able to catch a glimpse into the life of a child for whom the world is an overwhelming and often frightening place. Kids he didn't even know started saying hi, and after school one day, Daniel said, "Mom, I like myself."

Dani was later asked to give a workshop for teachers and parents. She also returned to Daniel's class mid-year to ask how things were going and to answer any questions the students had about him and his habits, abilities, and behaviors. Together, they brainstormed a few catchy responses they could use when other students made negative comments about Daniel.

At the end of the year, Daniel's family threw a party for the class. The cake had a rainbow and said, "Friends make life special." Dani took her camera and a few rolls of film to take "friendship photos." Then she made copies so each child could take pictures of their friends home for the summer. Almost everyone wanted a picture taken with Daniel.

Being an Ambassador

Advocacy also means helping build others' awareness of special-needs children. "With my son in a wheelchair, I feel I'm almost doing a public service announcement," says Dara Howe. When they're at the mall or in a restaurant, people sometimes look at him with sadness, thinking, *What a pity—a little boy who can't run, walk, or talk.* They look at his mother and search her face for how she's handling his disability. When her actions and expressions project, "We're coping; we're a regular family, happy and well-adjusted," people get a positive sense, and it takes some of that pity away.

When little children come up and say, "Why can't he walk?" Dara realizes they're just being curious, and she uses that encounter to help them understand that the wheelchair doesn't confine him but allows him to go places and do things just like other kids.

Home Schooling Special-Needs Children

As their child's advocate, some parents choose home schooling as the best and least-restrictive environment for education. They may feel they know the most about their child's learning style and the best ways to address it. Many want a Christian education for their child. They may be able to offer more challenge and more one-to-one teaching and so help their child make more progress, especially if the special education program in their public schools is overcrowded. In some cases, a medically fragile child or one with a weak immune system needs to be home schooled to protect his health. Or the parents may choose home schooling because, despite their best efforts, they can't get the kind of education they feel their child needs in the public schools.

Parents are home schooling kids with all kinds of special needs and in a variety of ways: with the parents teaching, with a tutor who comes into the home, or through early intervention or other services of the public school district.

Of the approximately 1,000,000 families now home schooling, about 100,000 of them have children with special needs. Many of them do not take SSI or other governmental services for therapy, and thus they save taxpayers a conservative estimate of $70 million annually just in education costs.

Tom and Sherry Bushnell of Olalla, Washington, are one of those families. They home school their eight children, including three adopted ones: son Jordan, eight years old, who has Down syndrome; daughter Sheela, seven, who is blind; and daughter Sherlynn, their five-year-old who has severe cerebral palsy.

"One nice thing about home schooling versus outside education," says Sherry, "is that we don't have to deal with other people's biases or ideas about their disabilities. Children are going to pick up on those opinions about their capabilities or lack of them."

For example, their daughter Sheela, although blind, is very bright. Because of her disability, if she were in public school, she might be in a classroom with mentally impaired children and so be much more limited in her opportunities. "Right now she functions like any other seven-year-old because we've given her the opportunity and confidence to do things," Sherry reports. "She's doing well in school, uses a Perkins Brailler, and is a hands-on learner. She washes dishes, cares for the baby, and makes her bed just like the other members of the family."

The Bushnells also find that home schooling gives them the time and availability to work on godly character training and spiritual development with their kids. "Whenever we've asked for wisdom, whether that's for a medical or educational need, God has supplied it," Sherry says. Over and over, He has brought a resource or a person or tuned them in to what their children need. And they see God's faithfulness multiplied in the more than 8,000 families in the organization they direct, NATHHAN (National Challenged Homeschoolers Associated Network).

NATHHAN supplies resources and also matches families dealing with specific disabilities with other families who are home schooling a child with a similar disability. They also have a NATHHAN family camp, a catalog of materials and books for parents of special-needs children, and an encouraging, informative monthly newsletter. To contact them or to request a sample copy of the newsletter, call (206) 857-4257, fax (206) 857-7764, or write 5383 Alpine Road SE, Olalla, WA 98359.

Whether we're educating others or educating our child, it takes all of us working together—parents, teachers, therapists, special services workers, and churches—to provide experiences that enrich the lives of our special-needs children and opportunities for them to enrich our lives.

To summarize what it means to be your child's advocate:

1. Keep files and records on your child.

2. Don't be afraid to ask for a conference during the school year if you have a concern.

3. Share your ideas with the teachers. Give them suggestions, and let them know what works for you in dealing with your child at home.

4. Don't be intimidated by teachers. They may be the professionals, but you are the expert on your child.

5. Focus on one or two problems at a time, and break problems down into manageable pieces. Decide what steps are needed, and take one step at a time.

6. Join parent organizations and support groups.

7. Communicate with your child's teachers regularly, not just at the IEP meetings. Make sure you encourage them when you can, especially when you notice success.

8. When you attend a meeting, have questions and suggestions written down.

9. Take a friend, spouse, or support person with you to meetings so you don't feel alone.

10. Pace your time well during a meeting, because it's easy to run out of time.

11. Don't get defensive, even when you feel you're being attacked. Keep calm.

12. Make sure your child's IEP is going to meet her needs, not the teachers'. (Example: Don't settle for a curriculum of all functional-living skills and no academics if your child is capable of academics.)

Encouragement from Scripture

- "For the LORD gives wisdom, and from his mouth come knowledge and understanding" (Proverbs 2:6).

- "For nothing is impossible with God" (Luke 1:37).

- "I praise you, O Father, Lord of heaven and earth, for hiding these things from the intellectuals and worldly wise and for revealing them to those who are as trusting as little children" (Luke 10:21, TLB).

- "Call to me and I will answer you and tell you great and unsearchable things you do not know" (Jeremiah 33:3).

CHAPTER 8

PRAYER: A LIFELINE FOR PARENTS

It was Jay's first night on oxygen, and I (Louise) knelt by his bed and asked what he wanted to pray for. It was our usual routine, and he always had a request. Sometimes it was difficult to understand his speech, but with gestures and sign language, he always made his desire known. Often it was for his brother away at college or his grandparents. Tonight, however, he requested an angel.

As I prayed, my mind raced back to a day weeks earlier when Jay had told me about seeing an angel in his room.

"What did he look like?" I had asked.

Jay had wiggled his thumb and pinkie and signed, "Yellow."

"You mean the angel's clothes were yellow?"

"Yeah."

"What about his face and hair?"

Again he signed, "Yellow."

Suddenly I realized he had no way to say "golden," "bright," or "shining," so his description made sense. My son had seen an angel!

Soon Jay began to tolerate the oxygen, but his prayer request remained the same every night—an angel. "What he really needs is a friend," I told God, "a buddy to play with." Because of progressive heart disease, Jay was now schooled at home. Without classmates, he was isolated and lonely. It broke my heart to see him sitting in his room alone, playing with his G. I. Joes. But sometimes it seemed as if the toys played back. Once, I found a remote-controlled army tank rolling across his floor at 2:00 A.M., its red light flashing in the dark while Jay slept peacefully. My husband explained it away as having something to do with radio waves.

One special night, the room was quiet as I was putting Jay to bed. "Angel," he signed to me again. Then he looked intently toward the door and grinned. It dawned on me that he had been repeating this routine for weeks.

"Jay, what are you smiling at?" I asked.

He pointed.

I looked around, asking, "What is it? What do you see?" My son grew frustrated. "An angel?" I guessed.

"Yeah!" he replied. He motioned toward the door and animatedly explained that an angel stood by his door each night and sometimes spoke to him. Our prayers had been answered! What a gracious and loving heavenly Father to let a lonesome young man become friends with an angel, and a playful one at that! And what reassurance it is for me to be able to stop at Jay's doorway each night and ask this unseen warrior to watch over my son while he sleeps.

Answered Prayers

Just as God met Jay's request for an angel, He gives us as parents and children extra grace for the additional challenges and trials we face—not just once, but over and over. As we talked with dozens of parents, we heard how God brought peace to anxious parents in the waiting room while their child was in surgery. In response to a cry for wisdom, He brought just the right person and action plan another family needed for therapy. He opened doors to a group home situation when a family who moved to a different state had been told they would face a five-year wait.

God gave strength when a mom had been up so many nights with her sick child that she didn't know how she could go on. He supplied the money to pay a huge medical debt for a family that had no resources of its own. He showed another parent a creative way to develop empathy in her son's classmates when she prayed about how he'd be treated in a mainstreamed classroom.

Prayer makes a difference, because God cares. He cares about a special child's need for a friend. He cares about a child's respiratory infection and wants to bring His healing touch. His heart aches with parents when they hear discouraging reports from a doctor, and He hears the prayers of moms and dads for strength and wisdom. He even gives little ones another chance at life when there seems to be no hope.

Another Chance at Life

"When you're ready to take Taylor off the ventilator, we'll help you decide," said the nurse. Only two weeks earlier, Debra Williamson had held her adopted daughter in her arms right after delivery and thanked God for the child for whom she and her husband, Peter, had prayed.

However, only moments later, Taylor had been placed on oxygen because of "a little trouble breathing." Maybe pneumonia or a virus, the doctors had said. Her parents had been assured that lots of babies need help breathing at the beginning. But by the fourth day, Taylor's ability to breathe had deteriorated, and the physicians had recommended flying her to a neonatal intensive care unit in another city. There she had been given X rays, a battery of tests, and powerful antibiotics. A ventilator had begun pumping air into her diseased lungs, and a stack of machines had towered over her cradle.

Day after day, Debra had watched her baby and wept—she was hooked up to massive tubes and monitors, sedated into an induced coma, and unable to breathe on her own. Finally, a diagnosis was reached: pulmonary surfactant protein B deficiency, an inherited, extremely rare disorder. Debra and Peter had been told their infant had only weeks to live.

Nonetheless, they had firmly rejected the idea of taking Taylor off the ventilator, instead continuing to pray and search for what could be done. "She was our baby from the first moment she was put in our arms," says Debra. "I wouldn't have walked away from her any more than I would have from our biological child."

They learned that the only place in the country doing research on the disorder was Johns Hopkins Hospital, and in desperation they called the researcher who had discovered the condition in 1991. "Could there be some mistake? Would they retest?" the doctor asked.

The test was given again, and again the result was positive. The Williamsons were devastated. After crying what seemed like buckets of tears, they decided there had to be something that could be done for Taylor, and they pressed the researcher for more information.

"Well, I do know of two baby girls who received double lung transplants and survived," he replied.

After talking with the mother of one of the babies and, after much prayer, coming to grips with the fact that it was the only thing that could save Taylor's life, the Williamsons had her transported to Children's Hospital in Los Angeles. Four weeks later, after much anxious waiting, she received new lungs. The surgeon said that without the transplant, she would have made it only another week or two.

Three weeks after surgery, Taylor went home. Her dad had lost his job because of being at the hospital so much, but he found another one several months later. Today she's a happy, bright two-year-old who takes 40 doses of medication each day. Her parents don't know what the future holds, but they're grateful for each day with their daughter.

"Every day with Taylor is a blessing, a miracle," says Debra. "And having her is worth any sacrifice. We don't know what will happen in the future. She could reject the lungs tomorrow. The drugs are hard on her organs. Will she see her third birth-day? Her fifth? That uncertainty is the hardest thing, but we try not to dwell on it. We pray, and we put all our faith in God and hope He won't need her for a long time!"

A Prayer for Protection

Because Karen Wingate was visually impaired, she prayed each night that God would protect her toddlers in ways she could not. Her prayer was laden with emotions she couldn't express and filled with fear and a sense of inadequacy, knowing she couldn't protect her children as she thought a parent should. She was most afraid for daughter Christine, who is also visually impaired.

"I believe that sometimes God allows near-crises to happen to show us that He is, indeed, answering our prayers," says Karen.

One morning when Christine was barely two, she toddled into the kitchen. Her mother couldn't see that the coffeemaker had not yet been pushed away from the edge of the counter. Karen's back was turned as she sorted laundry on her kitchen floor. She turned around just in time to see Christine yank the coffeepot off the burner and fling it over her shoulder.

The glass shattered on impact. Since they were both barefoot, Karen scooped her toddler into her arms and then froze in front of thousands of sharp, unseen shards. Slowly backing out of the kitchen and then checking Christine all over for blood, Karen called a neighbor to help her clean up the broken glass.

While she waited for the neighbor to arrive, her prayer came back to her. God had, indeed, protected her daughter in a way she could not, for neither of them was hurt.

Yet another time, Christine fell into a deep swimming pool. A friend turned around just in time to see her plummet to the bottom and reacted so quickly that Christine wasn't even sputtering when he heaved her out of the water. Karen's prayer came back to her again: "Lord, please protect them in ways I can't."

While the challenges of keeping children safe might be greater for a physically challenged mom, Karen came to realize that no parent can keep her child perfectly safe. We must *all* rely on God to protect our children.

"My guiding light has been the words of Henry Ward Beecher, the founder of Perkins Institute for the Blind and a proponent of physical education for the handicapped," says Karen. "'Better to suffer the bumps and bruises of activity than to suffer the rust of inactivity.' Our physically challenged children need to be allowed to explore, move, flex, and use their bodies. It's my faith and my daily prayers for her safety that help me to let go of my daughter."

The Prayer of Release

Richard Foster says in his book *Prayer* that as we pray the prayer of relinquishment and release our concerns, the situation, or our children to God, we begin to enter into a grace-filled releasing of our will and a flowing into the will of the Father (*Richard Foster,* Prayer *[New York: Harper Collins, 1992],* p. 47). But this relinquishment is not without great struggle. Often we try to handle everything ourselves.

When Joan Consiglio's daughter Abby became disabled at five months of age, Joan and her husband felt that God had somehow let them down. Thinking He was unwilling to look out for the best interests of their baby, they decided to take up the slack.

"It was a whole seven months later that I finally had come to my end—I'm very stubborn—and Abby was near death," says Joan. "There was no way I could help; God had to do something new or take her home. I was even foolish enough to think I had to beg Him to get moving!"

As she entrusted her baby's life to God, He patiently and tenderly showed her that although she was the hands and feet making the motions, *He was* taking care of Abby. Abby lived, and more than seven years later, God is still the one taking care of Abby even as her mom feeds her, gives her medication, and sits at the computer with her. Knowing this, Joan can seek His advice on everything from how to help Abby swallow to what English curriculum to use in home schooling her.

In releasing Abby to the Lord, Joan's most important

Prayer and Baseball

As a child, Shane Whitworth, a young man with Down syndrome, wanted to play baseball. His mom, Pat, would watch him throw the ball up in the air and swing the bat over and over, never once hitting the ball.

One day, near tears and in desperation, Pat ran outside, praying as she went, "O God, You know how badly this little boy wants to be like other boys. Just once, please let the ball and bat connect, and let him feel the thrill of hitting a ball!"

Pat picked up the ball and tossed it to Shane. He swung the bat and hit the ball on his first attempt, sending it high into the air and across the yard. "It almost seemed to be in slow motion so we could savor the moment," says Pat.

The whole incident lasted less than 15 minutes and took place years ago. But Pat still remembers the joy she felt that day for her son and for the immediate answer to her prayer.

"The fact that the Lord of this universe heard the desperate plea of a mother to see her son hit a ball was one of the most awesome spiritual experiences of my life," she says. "To me, it was a miracle!"

discovery—the one that has restored her joy—has been the realization of how very much He loves her daughter. And she has learned that in every difficulty, if she will only wait on Him, He will supply the answer to their dilemma *(Joan Consiglio, "But God,"* NATTHAN NEWS, *summer 1996, pp. 29-30).*

Depending on the Holy Spirit When We Pray

"Many times when Eric is fussy or ill, we don't know where he hurts, and he can't tell us," says his mother. Since Eric speaks only a few basic words, it can sometimes be a real guessing game to figure out what's wrong. His parents have had to rely on the Holy Spirit numerous times to give them wisdom to know what to do for him.

James 1:5-6 encourages us to ask for wisdom: "If you don't know what you're doing, pray to the Father. He loves to help. You'll get his help. . . . Ask boldly, believingly, without a second thought" (THE MESSAGE).

Another family has an 11-year-old daughter who is multi-handicapped. She has no speech and no way to communicate. For two months, the little girl had episodes of terrible pain. Her parents took her to the pediatrician several times, but he found nothing that would cause that kind of pain. Her suffering continued. The parents prayed and prayed. They took her to healing services at their church and asked for special prayer. Another trip to the doctor proved fruitless. After more prayer, they finally thought to take her to the dentist, who discovered she had two bad teeth. They'd had no idea! Since she's fed by a gastronomy tube, she never eats by mouth. Once the two teeth were extracted, their daughter was back to her happy, cheerful self.

We need the Lord's wisdom when we pray for our children! That's always true, but it's especially the case when they can't tell us what's wrong.

God's Preparation

When Vicki Calason thinks of her son Ryan, age 15, she thinks of Hannah's prayer: "For this child I prayed" (1 Samuel 1:27, KJV). He is her firstborn, and he was definitely prayed for! When Vicki was pregnant, she and her husband happened to study a lot about how Jonathan's son Mephibosheth was taken care of by King David and fed at his table because of Jonathan and David's covenant.

Then when their baby boy was born with spina bifida, which caused crippling in his legs and feet in addition to other problems, they felt comforted and knew that God would always take special care of Ryan. Even before he was born, God got their attention and prepared them for what lay ahead.

When God's Answer Is Different
from Our Request

In January 1989, Katie Young's parents heard about a research program being run at the Rett Center in Houston for an experimental drug that seemed to have promise. They began to pray and asked their friends at church to pray that Katie would be accepted into the program. Meanwhile, they prepared a video and her medical records and went through the time-consuming process of applying.

When the answer came that Katie's level of functioning was too low for her to be chosen for the study, they were devastated. "We had accepted that she was different and handicapped," says her mom, Dottie. "But it was awful to think that here in this group of other children with the same disability, she functioned too poorly to fit the protocol."

However, the researchers told them Katie could participate in one phase of the testing. Her parents decided that even this limited participation might yield information that would be helpful to their daughter, so Katie and her mom flew to Houston for a long week of tests at the Texas Children's Hospital. They requested prayer specifically for Katie to be calm and peaceful.

"It came as no surprise that Katie's week was characterized by those two very traits—calmness and peace," Dottie says. "She wasn't extra cheerful, but she was very patient through all the painful testing. God's answers to prayer are so very real and concrete!"

And the drug study? Katie's parents got special permission to give their daughter the new medication and be monitored by her local doctors. That way, Katie avoided numerous trips to Houston and had the best situation possible.

"We praised God for His provision," says Dottie.

Sometimes we put our prayers in packages because we think we know how things ought to be done, but God can look at the real need and then answer with what's best.

Praying for Your Child in School

Prayer also makes a tremendous difference for our children in school challenges and changes. When Carrie Sisler was in junior high, her parents were told their daughter's special education class would have a change of teachers. Carrie, because of a severe reaction to the MMR vaccine (measles, mumps, rubella) at 16 months of age, had become mentally handicapped and subject to seizures. Every year, her mom, Paula, prayed fervently that God would provide a loving teacher, and this year was no exception.

When school started, the teacher assigned to Carrie's class seemed an ideal match. All year long in her daily time with God, Paula prayed for this teacher. She also bathed the class, Carrie, and her teacher in prayer in her weekly Moms in Touch group. Although not a Christian, the teacher seemed to have a heart for the students and was a good role model. As a result, Carrie had a good year and made progress.

The next year, Carrie moved up to the next level of special education, and her teacher from the year before was with a different class. Before long, Paula began to hear reports that this teacher was being abusive toward her students, who were becoming afraid to go to school. The teacher was finally removed from the classroom.

"We found out later that this behavior was more consistent with the teacher's career—she had shown abusive behavior before—but none of that surfaced the year Carrie was in her class," Paula reports. "All we could see is that as we covered Carrie and the class in prayer, God put a hedge around them to protect them."

Praying with Other Parents

The first time a group of mothers gathered to pray as "Moms in Touch" for McCoy Elementary School in Carrollton, Texas, five women came to spend the hour together. As it turned out, four out of the five had children with some kind of special need or disability.

"I'll never forget that day as long as I live," says Martha Little, who had gone to the meeting reluctantly that day to pray for her son Max, who has brain damage and struggles with many learning problems. "Huge burdens were lifted. As we prayed together, lifting each child up, we were bearing each other's burdens."

The women cried and cried. The mascara ran. Several had never had another parent pray with them for their child. And for a year and a half, until the kids graduated from middle school, those moms prayed together weekly—for the principal, the teachers, their own children, and their classmates. (*To contact Moms in Touch, call 800-949-MOMS.*)

Let Scripture Guide Your Prayers

Daily Bible reading is a great help in praying effectively for our children. When we pray Scripture, we find increased faith and confidence in God's promises. Fear and anxiety leave and are replaced by peace.

Following are some Scripture-based prayers to pray for children with disabilities and for yourself. They're helpful whether you're praying in a parents' support group or a Moms in Touch group, on your own, or with a partner. Pick a verse each week to pray for your child, or put stars by the ones that strike you as applicable to the need. Letting Scripture guide your prayers is powerful: God's Word does not return void—it's a promise (see Isaiah 55:11)! (*Our thanks to Martha Little for compiling many of the scriptures and scriptural prayers.*)

Prayers for Our Special-Needs Children

Psalm 139:13-15: That they, and we, may know that our children are fearfully and wonderfully made, and that God's works are wonderful.

John 9:1-3: That they can grow to see their disability as a way God can be displayed and glorified in their lives.

2 Corinthians 12:7-10: That they would dedicate their weaknesses to Him so they can use them as opportunities to show His strength. Also, that they would be content with their weaknesses, with their insults (mistreatment), with their distresses, with their persecutions, and with their difficulties; because when they are weak, then they become stronger in the Lord.

Philippians 4:8: That they would learn to focus on the good, true, noble, right, pure, and lovely things about themselves, not just on their handicap or their disability.

2 Corinthians 1:3-4: That they wouldn't be too absorbed with their difficulties but would learn to reach out to others with difficulties or trials (whether they be similar difficulties or not).

Romans 12:4-6a: That they would find their own gift in Christ's Body early in life.

Isaiah 40:29-31: That they wouldn't grow faint or weary—that the Lord would renew their strength daily.

Psalm 119:99; 19:7: That they—especially those with mental handicaps and learning problems—would gain godly wisdom (not just the world's knowledge) through their studies.

Psalm 22:24; 62:8: That they would learn to cry to the Lord for help and, with the assurance that He hears their cries, would pour out their hearts to Him.

Philippians 4:6-7: That they would learn not to be anxious but to pray and bring their requests to God, and that they would experience His peace.

Romans 5:3-4: That God would build character in their lives through their disabilities.

Prayers for Our Children in Times of Illness, Surgery, or Other Crises

Psalm 91:11: Believe the promise that angels will protect them wherever they go, and pray for a surrounding of angels.

Romans 8:26: Thank the Holy Spirit for interceding for them when they're sick or have a need, even when you don't know how to pray for them yourself.

Hebrews 7:25: Jesus lives to make intercession for us. Remind yourself that He is interceding on behalf of our children and us for all our needs.

Psalm 112:7: Thank God for taking care of us, so that we have no need to fear bad news or live in dread of it.

James 5:14: According to this biblical instruction, we shouldn't hesitate to call our church elders or a strong individual Christian to pray for them and anoint them with oil when they're sick.

Matthew 18:19-20: Because there is power in numbers when

praying, we can ask others to pray with us. But even if we're praying alone from a human perspective, Jesus and the Holy Spirit are praying with us.

Psalm 34:4: Ask for deliverance from fear in raising them and being able to release them to God.

Prayers for Our Children Concerning Classroom and Peer Issues

Matthew 5:44: That they would learn to pray for those who intentionally or unintentionally hurt them.

1 Peter 2:23: When others taunt or tease them, that they would remember the example Christ gave us.

2 Corinthians 7:6: That when they get depressed, God would comfort them.

Romans 8:18: That they would have an eternal perspective and not get weighed down by the day-to-day tasks.

2 Chronicles 20:12-24: That they would learn to focus on God instead of their circumstances.

Prayers for Ourselves and Other Parents

James 1:19: That we would be quick to listen, slow to speak, and slow to become angry.

2 Chronicles 20:15: That we would remember this truth: "For the battle is not yours, but God's." Many times as parents, we need to be reminded of that! That we would recognize our own limitations and draw our strength from the Lord (see Psalm 73:26).

Romans 15:5: That we would turn to the Lord for endurance and encouragement, both for ourselves and for our children.

2 Corinthians 10:5; Matthew 6:25-34: That we would not be anxious about the unknown—the "what if's" or the tomorrows—but take every worry captive to the obedience of Christ.

Romans 8:28: That we would know that God weaves all things together into a pattern for good for those who love and trust Him.

Colossians 3:21 (TLB): That the Lord would give us discernment about when to scold and when our children's disabilities keep them from accomplishing something. We don't want them to become discouraged and quit.

Philippians 3:13b-14: That we would forget mistakes we've made with our children and press on.

Proverbs 28:13: That when we make mistakes, we would model openness by confessing them to our children or their teachers.

Praying for the Education of Special-Needs Children

The following suggestions can be useful in prayer groups or your own devotional time as God leads.

What to Pray for Nationally

Pray for proper programs for students with disabilities. Costs are high; pray for innovative ways to serve special-needs students while keeping expenses down. Pray also for a system of accountability so we can better assess the programs for special ed students. Pray for the process of identifying students with disabilities, especially for students who fall in the gray areas and aren't really getting the help they need because they can't get admitted into the programs.

Pray that Christian schools would become better equipped to deal with disabled students.

What to Pray for on a District Level

Pray that administrators would select good workshops for their classroom teachers so they will be better able to deal with the needs of disabled students, and that the workshops would teach godly principles.

Pray that programs would be available for all special-needs students in your district, and that these programs would help all children develop to their fullest potential.

What to Pray for at the Local Level

Pray for wisdom for doctors, therapists, technicians, and child-care workers. Pray that the teachers would properly modify curriculum. Pray also for a spirit of unity between parents and teachers concerning the students' needs. Pray for proper training for the teachers so they will be equipped to help their students; that they would not get frustrated when some children can't do things as quickly as others; that they would concentrate on the students' strong points and not just their weaknesses. Especially for the special education teachers, pray for patience and reliance on God's strength, and for loving speech to proceed from their mouths.

Finally, pray for the diagnosticians: that they would have godly insight into the needs and abilities of the students they're testing; that they would schedule evaluations for students at appropriate times; and that on testing day the students would be healthy and alert.

Encouragement from Scripture

- "As soon as you began to pray, an answer was given" (Daniel 9:23).

- "And we are sure of this, that he will listen to us whenever we ask him for anything in line with his will" (1 John 5:14, TLB).

- "Do not be anxious about anything, but in everything, by prayer and petition, with thanksgiving, present your requests to God" (Philippians 4:6).

- "For the Lord is watching his children, listening to their prayers" (1 Peter 3:12, TLB).

- "So let us come boldly to the very throne of God and stay there to receive his mercy and to find grace to help us in our times of need" (Hebrews 4:16, TLB).

CHAPTER 9

TIES THAT BIND: STRENGTHENING YOUR MARRIAGE

One of the most important things you can do for your children is to love your spouse. Yet couples with a disabled child divorce at a considerably higher rate than the rest of the married population (ranging from an 85% divorce rate to 10 times the normal rate). That's probably due to some special stresses: financial strain; the lack of time together as a couple; the fact that men and women grieve differently; and the incredible ongoing demands of caring for a disabled child. How can you and your spouse defy those odds and build a strong, loving, and mutually supportive relationship? Let's look at how some other couples have done it.

Home Alone

At 10:00 P.M., Tim dragged in from a long day at work and extra hours on his second job. Nancy, his wife, met him at the door, holding their son, who was fussy and feverish.

"I've had it!" she exploded. "I'll go get three jobs, and you can go sit instead of me while they're hooking Donny up to electrodes, he's crying, and I have to listen to more bad news from the test results."

Handing their son to Tim, Nancy wiped tears of frustration from her face as she collapsed on the couch. She had spent the afternoon at the doctor's office with Donny, who has severe cerebral palsy, a seizure disorder, and other problems. All she'd heard from doctors lately were negative reports that kept her on an emotional roller coaster.

After hours at the doctor's office, she'd had to pick up George, their other son, from school, fix the kids' dinner, feed Donny, supervise George's homework, and do therapy with Donny before getting them to bed. She was simply "mom-myed out" and at the end of her physical and emotional strength.

"You've got the harder job by far," Tim admitted as they talked. "It's easier for me to work all the time and be away than to deal with the pain of a handicapped child I can't fix."

Nancy felt that her husband was never home, that she was handling the parenting of both boys all alone. And Tim, like many men, was finding sanctuary in his job.

Their blowup, although unpleasant, brought the beginning of a new mutual understanding and a realization that although some aspects of the situation were out of their control, they could do a few things to alleviate Nancy's stress and work together more.

First, Tim began making an effort to join Nancy for Donny's doctor's appointments.

Second, they started "splitting Saturdays" to give each of them time out. Each parent got from 8:00 A.M. to 1:00 P.M. or 1:00 P.M. to 6:00 P.M. on Saturday to do whatever he or she wanted. Tim might fish at the lake; Nancy could have breakfast with a friend or do errands.

"I knew that on Saturdays I could count on five hours to myself, and it made a big difference," she says. They found they were better parents when they got those breaks.

Breaks *together* as a couple are also important, but sometimes they're hard to come by. Many marriages get the crumbs of a couple's time. Donna and Alan Johnson experienced financial pressure because of their son Eric's medical bills. They went more than six years without even a weekend trip apart from their children. With tensions rising, their pastor encouraged them to get away as a couple for regular dates, but they always answered, "We can't. We don't have the money."

"Ask God to provide a way," he urged them. And as they prayed, God did provide, sometimes in surprising fashion. Those once-a-week dates, on which they had a self-imposed rule of *not* talking about the kids, helped renew their relationship. Then when they had a decision to make concerning Eric or an upcoming IEP meeting, they set aside time to discuss what needed to be done.

It's difficult to go without any breaks. "You end up resenting your children and having problems with your spouse because you never have time," says Donna. Having seen how much their marriage was helped by time out as a couple, she started a respite care ministry at their church so other parents of special-needs children could also get a break.

Meaningful breaks won't happen for most couples, however,

unless they plan ahead for them. One couple combined their birthday presents and bought season tickets for the musical theater in their city. Schedule in hand, they planned ahead for a baby-sitter for their disabled child. They enjoyed the performances so much that the next year, they also got Sunday matinee tickets for their adult sons. This time out with their sons made some special memories.

Martha and her husband, Bill, a Texas couple, collect coffee antiques and once or twice a year go antiquing together. "He's a banker who gets those weird federal holidays that a lot of other businesses don't get, so we take those days to do something together, like antiquing," she explains. They also like taking drives in the Texas hill country. "We need time away, just the two of us," Martha says, "away from the rat race that bogs us down and from the mounds of homework that our son Max usually has because of being a slow learner."

Another couple, the Steigers, get out once a month, and four times a year they enjoy an overnight together while their children are at a friend's house having pizza and a video movie night. It's an adventure for their kids and much-needed time away for mom and dad. If money is short, they enjoy take-out food and time at home by themselves, perhaps just sitting up in bed and reading their catalogs or a long-neglected book.

Dani Steiger, the wife, has found that with three children, one of whom has special needs, this time away doesn't happen if it's not on the calendar. So she and her husband go out for a New Year's Day brunch each year and take along their organizer books. There they schedule once-a-month dates with each other and with the children (at the park, at the movies, etc.) for the entire year.

"Every time I open my organizer, there's a heart drawn on that day of the month coming up next, and it's something I look forward to," Dani says. "We find that when we know we're going to work on our relationship, other things fall into line. I know how he feels, and we're in this together. If we didn't have any dates set, I might feel bad when he works late for several nights in a row and I'm suffering cabin fever with the kids. He has his job and I have mine. On the weekends, he takes over the kids and fixes Saturday morning breakfast with my help."

When Having a Date Is Difficult

Parents with medically fragile children, with children who have certain disabilities, or with adult special-needs children often find it hard to locate responsible help so they can go out as a couple. They may have no family members close by whom they can count on to baby-sit.

Teresa Pickle and her husband, for example, experienced this because they have three children, two with cerebral palsy (ages 17 and 25 at the time of this writing) and serious medical needs who require a lot of care and lifting. How do they cope? At least once a week, the children go to bed early, and Teresa and her husband have "couple time." They may watch TV, hold hands and read, or talk, but it's a set time for the two of them. "We hunt for times for us," she says. "You can get a lot out of even 15 minutes together."

Sometimes they meet for lunch while the children are at school. They have also hired for an evening one of the habilitation training specialists who comes into their home to work with their boys. That frees them to go to a concert together.

As the Pickles have seen, sometimes therapists or in-home nurses who already know the child and his routine can be the best baby-sitters. In-home respite care is provided in most states for families with a disabled child. (The funding comes through regional centers such as the county health department, crippled children's medical services, etc., and parents need to ask what respite care is available.) In one family's case, for instance, they're allotted funds to pay for 96 hours a year of in-home baby-sitting; the parents are responsible for finding and hiring the person. *Ask, ask, ask* until you get the respite services you need.

Happiness Is Being Married to Your Best Friend

For Judy and Robert Stipes, some time away came as the result of an unexpected surgery. One of the difficult things Judy had felt throughout the years of mothering their son, Wesley, who has multiple handicaps, was that there was never any spontaneity. She's a spontaneous person, but she couldn't just hop up and take a walk with her family or run out for ice cream. Everything took extra planning, and even on an extended trip, they had to keep to the strict routine they followed at home.

"I had to think, *What can I feed him here? Can we get the wheelchair in here?*" she says. "Traveling with Wesley was very hard."

But when Wesley was 12 years old, he had extensive hip surgery near their home in Oklahoma City. After the surgery, he would be in a body cast, and his mother wouldn't be able to lift him. The doctors recommended a brief stay at the J. D. McCartey Center in Norman, a short-term residential facility 30 minutes away, where he could heal from the surgery and have all the physical therapy and rehabilitation he needed.

"I thought, *I can't do this because I can't be away from Wesley that long. I don't think we can possibly leave him,*" says Judy.

But when they visited the center and saw the full staff and only 20 or 30 children, plus an Olympic-size swimming pool for daily therapy, they chose to place him there from April to August. At the same time, they decided to make the best of the time and enjoy it.

Judy visited her son almost every day, but she also found it was a marvelous time to strengthen her marriage and her relationship with their daughter Rebekah. The three of them did spur-of-the-moment things like eat breakfast at a restaurant or go with friends for lunch after church, something not possible when Wesley was home. They even took a one-week vacation to Mexico, during which he was visited daily by an aunt.

"Robert and I both knew we needed this break," says Judy. "The mother focuses so much on the child that it can cause the husband to feel in second place and begin to resent it. It's normal to put the child at the top because he's hurting, but I also found I needed to take time to nurture our marriage—time for my husband and my other child."

Judy and her husband still enjoy each other after 30 years of marriage. In fact, Judy has a plaque she crosstitched that says, "Happiness is being married to your best friend."

Husbands and Wives: Grieving Differently

Another problem couples often face is that men and women grieve differently. This grief is not a one-time experience in many cases, either, but ongoing. If one of their parents died, the spouse could be strong and supportive. But when the grief is over a child, both parents are affected.

When we grieve for a child, we move through phases of denial, anger, bargaining, and depression before we come to acceptance and release. And this happens not just once, but again and again. Typically, however, husband and wife are at different points on the journey, and that can cause conflict.

"In grieving, if I'm in depression and my husband is in anger, we can't help each other," says a mother of three, one of them severely handicapped. "I want him to comfort me in my sadness and down times, but if he's angry, he doesn't have any patience with me. In fact, it seems as if he doesn't care."

With a disabled child, you suffer the loss of hopes, dreams, and expectations for your child and the future, say Norm and Joyce Wright in their book *I'll Love You Forever* (*Focus on the Family, 1993*). "Seeing the baseball glove purchased prior to birth now sitting in the disabled child's room, never to be used, may affect the athletic father more than the mother," they wrote. The mom may grieve for the things she won't be able to teach her child, the talks they can't have, the wedding she will never attend, or the suffering the child endures in surgeries.

The way spouses express grief may be poles apart as well. Men often don't cry or talk about it as readily as their wives, and they may have difficulty reaching out for help. Their tendency is to take action, to try to fix things, and they get frustrated when they can't. But when a man is silent, his wife ends up feeling alone and uncomforted in her grief. This pain, if not shared or talked about, can bring increasing distance between the two.

"Husbands and wives need to understand the grieving process," wrote the Wrights. "They may be in a continual state of grieving during the child's whole life and not in touch with what it takes to recover." Those who do recover deal with their feelings, communicate with their spouse, and have other people to help and support them.

"If you're only communicating with yourself, it's self-defeating," the Wrights add. "You keep passing on misinformation to yourself. It's vital that men tap into their feelings and talk about them."

Communication: Building Your Marriage

"From the beginning, we were very open and shared the discouragements and disappointments," says Carrie, the mother of a child with a genetic condition. In their case, Larry, her husband, is the stronger communicator. He was able to draw things out of Carrie and help her look at their son's situation more positively so she could gain perspective. At the same time, he didn't hide his own feelings of loss.

When Carrie was dealing with disappointment, guilt over being the carrier of the genetic condition, and fear about the future, the communication between her and her husband and the encouragement he gave were crucial. As a result, they are emotionally closer as a couple, and she didn't feel isolated.

Communication Tips

In many marriages, communicating feelings is a struggle. Here are some ways to keep the lines open, even during stressful times:

(1) If what you hear at a doctor's appointment is overwhelming or hard to deal with, give each other some space and time to process it before you talk. If your husband isn't ready, let him think about it. Before he leaves for work, you might say, "Tonight after Paula goes to bed, let's talk about this. I have some concerns I'd like to discuss with you."

(2) Take the pressure off ahead of time by explaining expectations. A man may avoid talking about a subject because he

feels he has to offer a solution to the problem, whereas his wife may really want a listening ear, acknowledgment that her feelings are valid, some compassion, a hug, and for him to just "be there." If she only wants him to be a sounding board and doesn't expect him to solve the problem, letting him know that may be a relief and open up communication.

(3) It's important for both husband and wife to understand you will handle anxiety, anger, and stress differently. Respect your spouse's way of coping, and don't try to change him or her.

(4) Taking a daily short walk together can also help keep communication channels open. Be each other's best friend. When a lot of negative reports and painful experiences are coming at us at once, we tend to take it out on our spouse; he or she may get the blunt end of our frustrations. Stop and take some deep breaths; remember that your spouse isn't the enemy, and think, *Would I treat a close friend this way?*

(5) Realize what your spouse's main mode of communication is, and reach out to him or her with that. If it's reading, write him letters or notes. If it's speaking or physical affection, allow time for that. For example, one wife realized that when her husband talks, he uses many analogies. She found that when she could give him an analogy or word picture, the light bulb would go on in his mind, and he understood her better.

(6) Tip from a husband: If you want your guy to talk, get him out of the house and do something fun, like eating out or seeing a movie. Then watch your communication open up.

(7) Sometimes the best way to communicate as a couple is through prayer. Ask, "How can I pray for you? What are you stressed about? What's your greatest need today, and how can I pray about it?" Then take a few moments to pray, either aloud or silently, for your spouse. This practice can bring enormous

comfort. Praying together enhances intimacy and strengthens your marriage. And just knowing you're carrying his or her burden to God when you also are in a difficult time can minister much love.

A Movie Breaks Through

Sometimes communication can open up in unexpected ways. In Dani and her husband's case, it was as they watched the movie *Forrest Gump*. They take turns picking what activity they will do on their once-a-month dates, and when it was Dani's turn to choose, she wanted to go see that movie. It was last on his list of things to do because he knew it was about a person with mental handicaps, but he went along.

In the scene where Forrest found out he was a daddy and saw his little boy for the first time, he immediately asked, "Is he smart?" At that point, Dani's husband started crying, and he didn't stop for 45 minutes. It was the first time he had opened up about his feelings. He described his disappointment that his son couldn't ever go to a prom or drive a car. He didn't know what to do with his expectations, or even how to be with Daniel. As they sat in their car in the parking lot, he wept and voiced his fears for Daniel. Once he expressed them, he asked his wife, "How do you handle this without being overwhelmed?"

"I just trust God," she said. "I know there's a place in this world for our child. I don't know how; I just know it." They had a breakthrough of understanding that night.

Thriving as a Couple

Here are some further ways that couples we interviewed build their relationship and their families:

Work together as a team. Norm and Joyce Wright learned how to work as a team and support one another in caring for their son, Matthew. Joyce took care of preparing meals and feeding Matthew, and Norm's job was cleaning up. Sharing the work in such a way prevents either spouse from burning out.

"It takes us an hour to get Jonathan dressed and ready for school in the morning," says Wayne Hardy. Wayne bathes and dresses Jonathan, and Lynette puts his braces on and feeds him breakfast. Then on Thursday evening, Wayne is with the boys while Lynette works at her part-time job at the public library. It's refreshing for her to focus outward for the hours she works at the library.

Besides engaging in joint decision making for Jonathan, Wayne goes to doctor's appointments whenever he can and takes Jonathan to one of his therapies each week.

"We go as a team whenever there's a decision to be made for Benjamin," says Barbara Graves. This is particularly important for IEP meetings. Barbara tends to get emotional when educators compare Benjamin (who has Down syndrome) to a child who functions at a normal pace instead of looking at his progress and how far he's come. But her husband, John, remains calm and more objective, so they balance each other out, confer together, and come up with the best possibilities for Benjamin's education.

Barbara and John also share some caretaking duties for Benjamin at home, but they didn't arrive at their present division of labor overnight. "You've got to determine times when Dad can be in charge at home so you begin to trust he can be there and take care of things," says Barbara. Although the father's boundaries may be different from the mother's, it can work.

"Mothers have trouble letting go and letting their husbands take over," Barbara continues, "but begin at the beginning to let him care for the child. Otherwise, you'll become a martyr, and he'll feel left out. Let Dad into the equation!"

Don't put off joy or time together. With six children, one of whom will probably live with them his whole life, John and Barbara see child-rearing as a lifelong occupation. "It's so important for us to live our lives not as 'Someday we're going to do ___ as a couple,' totally focusing on the kids and then someday focusing on us," she says. "For us this is a continuum, so we need to think of what we really want to do as a couple and how we're going to do it—instead of putting it off."

They find they have to somehow build time together into the system. When Barbara needed to go to a reading conference in Yosemite, for instance, John went along, and Grandma came and took care of the kids. For three days, while Barbara attended seminars, John rode his bicycle, and they were alone together at night. They've recently bought a tandem bike so they can ride together.

Grow in your faith together. "We pray together for each other and for our children," says Donna Johnson. If husband and wife stay in unity with the Lord, it's hard to go their own separate ways. Joint prayer is a hedge of protection in any marriage.

Donna also says she and her husband are "professional altar call participants." "We got prayed for a lot!" she says. "There were times I'd go to the altar and just say 'Eric.' That's all I'd have to say. I was grieving and hurt and was prayed for. A supportive church and friends make a big difference."

She and her husband have also taken many parenting and marriage classes. "We couldn't afford counseling, so marriage and parenting classes have strengthened our relationship and given us a springboard for discussion," she says.

Sarah Aldridge and her husband found that the pastoral counseling they got for the first year after their son was diagnosed with Down syndrome was a big support to their marriage.

Commitment

Many couples we interviewed said the secret strength of their marriage is a deep commitment. Diane Elliot, for example, says, "Being totally committed to our wedding vows which said, 'for better or worse, richer or poorer, sickness or health,' and realizing those vows encompassed the whole family and were made to God, has brought tremendous strength to our marriage."

Pam Whitley finds that trying to live out "the love chapter," 1 Corinthians 13, has strengthened her marriage. As she inserts her own name in the verses—"Pam does not hold grudges; Pam is kind and doesn't seek her own way . . . and accepts her husband as he is"—she finds her marriage enriched and her heart encouraged.

Shared worship is important to Norm and Joyce Wright, both at the church and at home on their own. As they listen to praise and worship tapes, watch Christian teaching videos, or read devotionals and inspirational materials aloud together, they experience a valuable bonding time.

For many couples, their shared love for their child is like a cement that solidifies their relationship. "Our child has done more to bind us together than anything else in our marriage," says Betty Keeton. "She loves us completely, and that was a precious binding factor to all of us."

A Support Network

The more varied your support network, the better it is for your marriage and family. A close friend to call and vent your feelings to on a difficult day, a supportive church, and helpful friends can make all the difference.

Support groups are valuable because you get to talk with people whose situations are similar to yours. (See chapter 3 for ideas on finding or starting a support group.)

Sometimes, however, friends and family members draw away because they're uncomfortable or don't know what to say or how to help. "Be assertive in telling your friends how to pray for you and what you need," advises Norm Wright. "Don't assume they know what you need. If you want the help, you must express needs, because nobody can read your mind. They don't know what it's like to parent a special-needs child." He suggests giving close friends and family a "road map" on how to minister to you by writing them a letter early in your child's diagnosis, explaining what the disability or medical problem is, how you're feeling, how they can help in practical ways, how much their prayer support would mean to you, and so on.

When people at Marilyn and Dave Talmadge's church in Kansas City said they wanted to pray for their baby daughter, Abby, born with Down syndrome and facing heart surgery, they made a laminated bookmark and gave it out. It was made of stiff cardboard and had a small color photo of Abby at the top. Below that was a list of concrete ways to pray for her surgery, her medical needs, and the family. People kept it in their Bibles as a reminder to pray.

The results were tremendous. "We felt an incredible prayer covering both as a family and over Abby's life," Marilyn says. "We could feel both a strong sense of God's presence and the practical effects of people praying."

Special Grace

What if you're reading this chapter and thinking, *That's fine for those couples, but my husband (or wife) isn't interested in working as a team or in spending time together as a couple.* Perhaps you're a mom who is shouldering the whole job of caring for your special-needs child and there's no husband with you in the day-to-day difficulties, hard work, doctor's appointments, and IEP meetings.

If you find yourself carrying the responsibility alone, God has extra grace for you. That's the testimony of Karen, the mother of a beautiful eight-year-old daughter, Sara, who is only 16 months old developmentally, nonverbal, autistic, and severely handicapped. With her husband busy in his career and three older children to care for, Karen found it a continuous sorrow that he focused on their healthy children while leaving the major care of Sara to her. He was a good husband and a caring father in many ways, but he wasn't in the trenches with her 50/50 with their special child.

For six years, she cared for Sara alone and continued to pray about their situation. One day, she was pouring out her frustrations to God again, and He began to speak to her heart about how He had made mothers with an especially nurturing spirit, and how dads generally take a more active role in their children's lives when they begin to talk. He encouraged her to look to Him instead of to her husband for help, and He reminded her of this verse: "No temptation has overtaken you but such as is common to man; and God is faithful, who will not allow you to be tempted beyond what you are able, but with the temptation will provide the way of escape also, that you may be able to endure it" (1 Corininthians 10:13, NASB).

In that moment, she was able to release her husband from

her expectations and let God take out all the stored-up anger she had toward him. The Lord also assured her He had other ways to provide the help she needed.

About that time, Karen had to have back surgery because carrying Sara for years had ruptured several disks. While Karen recovered, they found a college student who swapped a certain number of hours of child care each week for a room over the garage. Since then, her husband has always arranged to have a helper live above the garage. The 20 hours a week of help enables Karen to teach a Bible study and be involved in some community and school activities, thus adding balance to her life.

Her husband is also supportive emotionally. He still doesn't do the diapers, baths, or music therapy and one-on-one training an autistic child needs, but he nurtures his wife, and she nurtures Sara. One of their other children is especially loving and involved in Sara's life, too. As Karen has focused on what her husband brings to the marriage and on all the blessings God has provided, their family and her marriage have thrived.

"You can ruin your marriage by focusing on the lack, or you can bless your marriage by magnifying what's positive," she concludes.

Encouragement from Scripture

- "Let love and faithfulness never leave you; bind them around your neck, write them on the tablet of your heart" (Proverbs 3:3).

- "However, each one of you also must love his wife as he loves himself, and the wife must respect her husband" (Ephesians 5:33).

- "Be beautiful inside, in your hearts, with the lasting charm of a gentle and quiet spirit which is so precious to God" (1 Peter 3:4, TLB).

- "But remember that in God's plan men and women need each other" (1 Corinthians 11:11, TLB).

- "If you love someone you will be loyal to him no matter what the cost" (1 Corinthians 13:7, TLB).

CHAPTER 10

ALL ABOUT SIBLINGS

The situations and feelings that siblings of children with special needs face are as diverse as the families themselves. So many factors come into play: age, health, disability, temperament, and parental influence, for example. There is no perfect sibling relationship. Each is shaped by the different family members and surrounding circumstances. Some siblings feel extra stress at school, church, with their peers, or even at home; others hardly seem to notice there's anything unusual about their disabled sibling.

This chapter is not meant to give you a magic formula for sibling relationships. We hope, however, that some of the stories and tips will help to foster loving relationships between children with special needs and their siblings. You might also want to take advantage of various sibling support groups available in many areas. They could be a great benefit to the whole family.

Always a Hero

"One of the greatest things about growing up with Jay was just knowing he was a miracle child," says older brother Aaron. "Since the doctors gave us little hope of his ever growing into adolescence, it made me appreciate everything and every day. There's just no way to top that.

"My parents told me, soon after Jay was born, that he might not do things as quickly as other kids. I didn't think it was a big deal. He was just a baby. It wasn't like I was going to take him out to play football with my friends. But when he was two or three and he wasn't doing the things other kids that age were doing, it started to make sense to me. That's when I really knew there was a difference and got into studying genetics and giving reports in school so my classmates could understand Down syndrome.

"But Jay was always a lot of fun. He has an incredible imagination. There would be times when I would dress him up like a cowboy or a rock star just for fun. He would take on the persona of what he perceived that character to be, even though he may never have seen one. It's like he could live the fantasy, and I thought it was great."

As Aaron and Jay's mom, I (Louise) can attest to the creativity of their play. Although Aaron was eight years older and very responsible with Jay, I never knew what I would find when I walked in the door. One day I came home to find the whole living room made into a tent with blankets. They were inside with snacks, watching a video through one of the openings. Another time, Aaron strung fishing line across Jay's room and rigged a helicopter so the two of them could lie on the bed, pull a string, and watch the helicopter zoom to the center of the room. There it dropped a "bomb" onto a target made of blocks and books.

Today, Aaron is married to Amy and teaches art in the public schools. He's adamant that developmentally disabled students be placed in his classroom, and he really works at helping them grow toward their potential and be creative. "I'm extremely defensive of these kids," Aaron says, "and I have to watch that sometimes. If anyone says anything negative about them or just makes a comment about a child who is disabled, I take it as a personal insult against my brother."

Aaron describes life with his brother: "Jay brought a special closeness to our family that I can't explain. He treated everyone the same—unconditional love and acceptance. He just loves everyone. I never had a friend who didn't love Jay and enjoy being around him.

"Being with someone like that causes you to put your own priorities into perspective—the way one should be treated, what life is all about, and what's really important. Seeing that Jay's top three priorities were being happy, loved, and with his family caused me to reevaluate mine. And Jay is just fun to be around!"

Building Good Relationships

The things that grow healthy sibling relationships in families with special needs are the same as in any other family—love, respect, and encouragement, to name a few. And just as the parents' attitude toward a disability will set the tone for the rest of the family, so also a brother or sister's love and acceptance toward a sibling with special needs will provide a model for other children.

Parents can foster good sibling relationships by letting every child know he is loved individually for who he is. They can also encourage children to respect each other, which will discourage resentment toward the person with special needs.

Maybe you can identify with some of the following comments from moms about how their own children interact with each other:

- Stephen Pyne has two younger brothers and a younger sister. "Our second son has assumed the firstborn role," says their mom, Julie. "He has learned a sensitivity to those who aren't as good at things as he is. Steve has brought a dimension to our family that has been very good for the other kids."

- Kathy Runnals says her kids are just like other siblings: They fight continually but stick up for each other against other people.

- Jason Shanafelt has an older brother and two older sisters. "They have loved Jason from the start," reports their mom. "They sometimes have a better understanding of him and are more tolerant than I am."

- Sarah Aldridge says, "Our daughter, Emily, is 12 and a real advocate for her brother. She encourages six-year-old James to achieve lofty goals by teaching him in her own 'classroom.' She also teaches him horseback riding and how to sing along with the piano. But there is definitely some rivalry for attention at times, especially when the focus is totally on Emily."

- Martha Little reports that Abby and Max stick up for each other if someone is putting the other down, but at home you wouldn't know they care for each other.

A Normal Life

When Wesley Stipe, who has cerebral palsy, was six years old, his little sister, Rebecca, was born. His parents stopped at his school on the way home from the hospital so Wesley could do "show and tell" with her. So began a lifelong love between the two. As a baby, Rebecca learned to walk by pushing Wesley's wheelchair, peeping around the sides since she was too small to see over the top. As a toddler, she sat in her brother's lap while the family shopped. "He didn't have good use of his hands," says his mom, Judy, "but he would wrap his arms around his little sister and keep hold of her. She wasn't going anywhere!"

"I grew up thinking every house had a wheelchair," says Rebecca. "I spent a lot of time at Wes's school, so a lot of my friends were disabled. It all seemed normal to me. Once when I was about five, a girl from down the street came over and wanted to know what was wrong with my brother, and I said, 'Nothing.' It just never occurred to me that he was any different."

Rebecca even adapted her play toward the disabled. She had a life-size, floppy rag doll named Anna to whom she gave therapy daily as she had seen it done in Wesley's school. A senior in high school at the time of this writing, Rebecca has spent many hours in volunteer work with the disabled and plans to go into some kind of therapy as a vocation. She just hasn't decided which type she enjoys most.

"I think life with my brother has given me a better understanding of the disabled," she says. "I enjoy helping kids who are challenged and wish everyone could be exposed to this type of lifestyle and realize just how loving and 'normal' they are, no matter how 'different' they appear on the outside."

Special Sisters

Linda and Peggy Martin are more than just sisters; they're soul mates. Linda is in her fifties and has Down syndrome. Peggy, in her late forties, has Dystonia and is mildly developmentally disabled. Their mom, Winnie, says that while they were living at home, Linda was very loving, and Peggy kept everyone on the ball and alert about the weather.

When both women moved into the same intermediate-care facility, they were given separate rooms, but that didn't keep them apart. Since Linda had few communication skills and Peggy lacked none, Peggy camped out in her sister's room to be sure she was treated properly and to translate Linda's wishes to caregivers. If they didn't treat Linda according to Peggy's standards, she called her mom, who lived only minutes away. Winnie would either get on the phone or drive to the facility to take care of the problem. According to their mom, the girls have always had a special bond and understand each other without a spoken word.

Tender Love

Every night, Chris, 13 at the time of this writing, picks up his sister, 9-year-old Becca, and tenderly tucks her in bed. Although she's put in bed by her parents, she never stays. She gets up and wanders around, usually falling asleep on the floor beside her tape recorder.

Chris said to his mom recently, "Becca's been staying in bed more," sounding disappointed because he really enjoys tucking her in. "You know, Mom, Becca is the most important thing in the world to me."

"What do you mean?" Barbara asked.

"All I can say is she sure is easy to love," he replied.

Barbara saw his comment as a powerful picture of God's love for us. Just as this 13-year-old brother delights in his little sister, as different as she is—autistic, sometimes destructive, toddlerlike instead of being able to do the things normal 9-year-olds can do—God loves us in spite of all the crazy things we do because He set His love upon us.

Great Therapist

Brittany Townsend's brother, Brett, has always had a sense about what his younger sister needed. As a child, he loved to pull her around the house on a blanket. At the child study center, Brittany's parents were told to put her on a blanket on the floor and roll her from side to side to help improve her balance and give her a feel for where she was. Brett had already been doing it for months.

When the therapist told them to place Brittany on the bed and then push her over gently to help her learn to catch herself as a protective measure against face-forward falls, guess who had already been plopping her over on the bed? Big brother Brett.

"They have a wonderful relationship," says their mom, Tammy. "Brett and his friends love Brittany and give her lots of attention, but they never demean her in any way. When Brittany is sleepy or wants to cuddle, she will as likely go to Brett as to my husband Tim or me." Brett, who is five years older than Brittany, doesn't see it as a big deal. "Brittany is just Brittany," says Brett. "That's just the way she is."

Special Gift

When Audrey Alexander was born with spina bifida, her parents told big brother Greg, who was then three and a half, that God knew Audrey was going to face a lot of problems, so He gave her a great gift to help her—a sibling named Greg. Their mom, Stephanie, reports that Greg watches out for Audrey when they're with a group of children, but that when they're alone he doesn't let her get away with anything!

Puberty and Potty Training

"Madison, Madison, Madison! To Daisha it sometimes seems that everything is Madison," says Debra, mother of the two girls. "My phone calls about her, my meetings concerning Madison's education, her doctor visits and therapy appointments—they consume my life."

Daisha was an only child for eight years and enjoyed all the attention before her little sister with Down syndrome was born. And in Madison's three short years, she has undergone three surgeries, so Mom and Dad have had their hands full. When their schedules weren't so busy, Debra or Matt had a date night with Daisha every week by taking her to a movie or out to dinner. They aren't able to do this every week now, but they still try to schedule special time with their older daughter.

"We talk to her, pray with her, and listen," Debra says. "She knows Madison has special needs and can understand that. But sometimes, she isn't in a really good place emotionally. At 12, she's going through adolescence, and all those feelings of resentment and frustration sometimes come out. We let her vent those emotions as long as she does it in a respectful way."

In spite of some rough times, the family never seems to lose its balance. "If I survive puberty and potty training, it will be a miracle," Debra says with a laugh.

Daisha Becomes an Advocate

Though Daisha doesn't always like the extra time her little sister requires, she has always been loving and protective toward her. Now she's learning to become an advocate and tells her mom she understands more about why she has to spend so much time with Madison.

At school, two girls with disabilities attended Daisha's music class. Many times other kids would make fun of the girls, teasing them and calling them names. Though Daisha didn't like it, she was afraid to say anything, fearing the ridicule would turn on her. Finally, she came to a breaking point and called her mother from school in tears. "I can't take it anymore," she said. The two of them prayed together, and then Debra called the music teacher and asked her to please be sensitive to this issue, both for the girls involved and for Daisha.

A mother of one of the disabled girls heard of the incident and asked Daisha to accompany her to the counselor's office, where the matter was settled. The music teacher announced to the class that the ridicule would not be tolerated, and Daisha volunteered the information that her sister also has Down syndrome. "Daisha went from meek and mild to advocate," says Debra.

To show her appreciation for Daisha's kindness, the girl's mom sent her a thank-you note. She then called Debra and told about a conversation she'd had with her daughter. "Mom, do you know who Daisha is?" the girl had asked.

"Yes, I do," she'd said.

"She's my friend!"

Debra is proud that Daisha has spoken up for those who can't speak for themselves. "I believe God prepares our children to be siblings of children with special needs," Debra says. "They will be better people—become better wives, husbands, whatever—just better people."

Tips for Parents

- Give your children enough information to help them understand their sibling's disability. The ages of the children and the nature of the disability will be factors in how much information you need to convey.

- In every way possible, promote a typical sibling relationship, but don't expect it to be perfect. Tolerate some sibling rivalry.

- With all your added responsibilities, be careful not to neglect a child who is quiet and complacent.

- As much as possible, attend the siblings' school, sports, and church functions that you attended before your child with special needs was born.

- Give the siblings permission to have ambivalent feelings toward the child with special needs. In time, their attitudes will mature.

- Talk with older children to get their opinions about important decisions concerning their disabled sibling. They like to remain informed about what's happening.

- Don't always use an older child for a baby-sitter. But by the same token, don't deny her a responsibility that would be hers provided the younger brother or sister had no special needs.

- If at all possible, spend time alone with each child. Some focused attention to play a board game, take a walk, or throw a baseball in the yard can make a big difference. Affirm your love for them.

- Do things together as a family. Continue to pursue hobbies, attend sporting events, take family vacations, go to church together, go fishing, have a picnic, and so on.

Brother in Charge

When Charlie and Sandy Warren decided to go on a weekend marriage retreat, a friend offered to stay with their three children, including their daughter Jan, who is multihandicapped. One problem—the friend couldn't make it to the house until 4:30 P.M., and the Warrens had to leave at 8:00 A.M. Sixteen-year-old Todd was also away for the day, so that left 13-year-old Brad in charge of his sister.

Knowing Brad had never kept Jan that many hours before, Sandy "coached" him beforehand. "Brad, do you think you can handle it?" she finally asked.

"Sure, Mom," he answered. "She'll be fine. I'll just slide the food under her door!"

Everyone did survive the weekend, and today both of Jan's brothers are in college. Until recently, Todd was at a university only 30 minutes from home. Knowing Jan would miss her brothers, he made a point of visiting his little sister every Sunday afternoon.

"It would be different if Jan showed emotion," says her dad.

"But because of autistic tendencies, she didn't reward Todd with hugs, kisses, or even much of an acknowledgment of his presence." Still, Todd kept coming, and there were plenty of signs that let him know Jan was glad to see him, even if she didn't express it openly.

Creative Ideas

When Wade was in the fifth grade, his teacher introduced a health unit about genetics and began to talk with the students about people who have special needs. Wade volunteered that his brother, Ryan, had Down syndrome and agreed to give a report. He looked up all the necessary information about trisomy 21 (extra twenty-first chromosome) and gave a good report. But the greatest hit with the kids was a photo album of little brother Ryan.

The album started with baby pictures that showed Ryan's progress, such as crawling and walking, with his age under each picture. Wade also included cute pictures with funny captions under them, like one of Ryan screaming while getting his hair cut and another of him sitting in a box at Christmastime. The kids could see that Ryan's progress was, indeed, a little slower than that of most children, but the pictures showed that he liked the same things they did and was pretty much a regular kid. Afterward, the teacher wrote a note to the mom, telling her how much the whole class had enjoyed the presentation.

Show your children ways to be creative in educating their friends and classmates about their sibling's disability. Everyone involved will benefit.

Adult Siblings

Teresa Walters was 14 when her sister, Tiffany, was born. "She was so sweet, and at 23 she still is," says Teresa. "I've learned so much about being sensitive and loving from Tiffany, who is developmentally disabled. She cares deeply about her friends and family and loves blindly those who show her love."

Though Teresa now lives in Tennessee and Tiffany lives in Kentucky, Tiffany spends a week or so every year with her big sister. "The main things we get in are swimming, pizza, and a movie," says Teresa. "Once those three things have been accomplished, she's pretty happy just to be here."

Teresa has some helpful suggestions for siblings of adults with disabilities:

- Encourage them to learn how to be independent and to be as self-reliant as they can.

- Make sure they get as much education as possible.

- Affirm their new skills, no matter how small they appear to you. Learning new skills is a big accomplishment.

- Spend time with them, and enjoy their unique personality.

- Get them involved with people like themselves.

- Consider options for when your parents will no longer be able to care for them.

- Consider options for yourself, if you become the caregiver, for when you may no longer be able to care for them.

"I know my life would not be the same without Tiffany's influence," says Teresa. She believes Tiffany's example helps her to realize the following truths:

- How important friends and family are.

- How special Jesus is.

- How simple pleasures add such joy and depth to our lives.

- How important it is not to look at people superficially—at their looks, abilities or inabilities, color, or race.

"Tiffany helps me see people as children of God—people to accept and to learn from," Teresa says. "She has shown me how important it is to spend time with the people you love and care about. Give them a hug and let them know you're glad to see them." (*Adapted from* Special Education Today, *Baptist Sunday School Board, April/May/June 1996, pp. 16-17.*)

Bridesmaid

Kari Cole is the youngest of four children. Her parents were always involved in all the children's activities, so Kari was also involved. "She attended all our special events when she was young, so I think it's important that I do the same for her," says older sister Kandy, who tries to attend Kari's swim meets at Special Olympics. Kari also attends football games with her sister and brother and stays with them when their parents go out of town.

"Kari has a lot of nieces and nephews, and they all just love her," says Kandy. "My five-year-old daughter wants Kari to go with her everywhere. They're great friends."

Some of the highlights in Kari's life have been her siblings' weddings. She was a bridesmaid for both her sisters and a reception attendant at her brother's wedding. "She felt pretty special," says her mom. Kandy praised Kari as being a "real trouper," having to stand very still and in high heels for 30 minutes to an hour. "She was just glowing at my wedding. She even helped at the bridal luncheon."

Kandy feels Kari is a great blessing to their family. "She has such an innocent, sweet, pure love. It's just great to have the opportunity to see something like that."

Lighter Side

At age four, Rebekah Chaney, big sister to Leah, who has Down syndrome, asked her daddy if she would have a baby when she grew up. Her father answered, "Yes, if God decides to give you a baby."

Rebekah immediately asked, "Will my baby have Down syndrome?"

"Probably not," said her dad. "It's pretty rare."

Rebekah answered indignantly, "Why not?" She was disappointed she wouldn't have a baby just like her little sister.

Importance of Family

Before Katie was diagnosed with Rett syndrome, her parents decided to make her life, as well as that of her three brothers, as normal as possible. "We could have gone all over the country trying different programs," says Dottie. "But we made a conscious decision to value our family relationship over a relentless pursuit of answers." That doesn't mean they stuck their heads in the sand concerning her disability or quit looking for helpful programs, but they did not make the search for a diagnosis more important than their family.

When they found a diagnosis, the question was asked, "What's in Katie's best interest?" The answer was the same as before—keeping her in a family that loves her. "I feel Katie's greatest strength is being part of a normal family," says her mom. "Katie is not the center of the universe, with her brothers as satellites. Because of that, they love her and don't resent her." Katie's brothers realize she has special needs, but accommodating them has always been a part of their lives and seems perfectly normal to them.

Sandy Rios voices the same sentiment. Her daughter Sasha requires total care. Sandy cautions parents not to forget the bigger picture—other siblings: "The disabled child shouldn't be *everything*, with life revolving around her. You may feel that other children will understand, but in fact, they grow up feeling resentful and neglected." And she adds, "It's important to instill a sense of pride in siblings and help them celebrate the life of the child with special needs."

Tips to Share with Siblings

- Learn about your sibling's disability. Read books and ask questions.

- Learn to communicate with your brother or sister, whether it's with sign language, eye blinks, facial expressions, sounds, or some other system that will work for you.

- Be a good role model so your sibling will know how to act. Show good manners and social behavior, like being polite in public.

- As much as possible, include him or her when you play. Keep in mind that it's sometimes hard for a person with special needs to find friends.

- Offer to baby-sit your brother or sister on occasion if you're old enough.

- Try to find something that's really fun for your disabled sibling, and share that activity with him or her. Some suggestions: watching videos, working puzzles, building blocks, reading books, feeding birds.

- Realize that *all* younger brothers and sisters take extra time. Mom and Dad also spent a lot of time with you when you were little.

- Remember you are still very special to your parents. No one else will ever be like you.

- Trust that because God loves you and your sibling very much, He will show both of you the best way to love each other.

- From a 13-year-old comes this tip: "Just live with it!" Having a sister with special needs is no more a big deal for him than having two older brothers who always boss him around.

- Attend events that your brother or sister is involved in, such as Special Olympics.

- If you're an adult sibling, involve your brother or sister in special functions you plan, such as weddings and Christmas parties.

No Time from Mom

One of the hardest times for parents of children with special needs is when they have to spend extended time in the hospital with their child, and the siblings at home have to make it without Mom. It may be difficult for the siblings to understand why their mother isn't doing all the things she used to do and why she has to be gone so much. Each child will react differently depending on age, temperament, who's in charge at home, and how critical things are at the hospital.

Try to keep the siblings' routine as normal as possible. If they're school age and involved in outside activities, ask a friend to take them to their events if a parent isn't available. If the child with special needs is not in critical condition and the hospital is within driving distance of your home, the parents can take turns staying at the hospital so Mom can be home part of the time with the other children.

Perhaps someone from your church could bring siblings to the hospital for a visit and relieve the parents while they sit in the lobby with the children, walk outside, browse through the gift shop, or go to the snack bar and have a soft drink. Be as innovative as possible, but remember that God knows your situation and will give both you and your kids the grace to get through the crisis and remain a close, loving family.

Crucial Care

The needs of a child with severe medical problems can consume the lives of everyone in the family. Ben's health and immune system were so compromised from the time he was born that he could be in a crisis in minutes. His care required *all* his mom and dad's time. No time remained to attend soccer games or anything else for their other children, Kim and Chris. Ben's breathing treatments and other medical procedures had to be a priority, not to mention his numerous appointments with doctors two hours away—sometimes as many as four a week. One parent always had to be home with Ben, and since Dad's job frequently took him out of town, Mom was the caregiver. Other people always had to pick up Kim and Chris for different functions and then bring them home.

"There was no consistency with the other children," says Nancy, Ben's mom. "No regular bedtime; no particular time for dinner. Their friends couldn't come over because of Ben's suppressed immune system. I couldn't even read them a book. If I had a 20 minute window without Ben needing me, I was so exhausted that I had to lie down and rest."

This built resentment in Kim and Chris. Though Nancy felt bad for her two older children, her constant fatigue and lack of

From an essay written by Ben Whitley

If people only realized that having a handicapped child is not just something that happens to a child! It happens to a family. It's something that makes their life totally different from everyone else's. If they only knew!

energy sometimes gave way to impatience and a short temper.

Eventually, Ben had to be placed in a pediatric medical facility offering 24-hour-a-day care. The family visits Ben often. And as Chris and Kim mature and understand why Ben required so much of their parents' time, relationships have healed.

If you know a family whose lives are consumed by a child's medical needs, help them as much as possible. Cook a meal for the family. Take the other children to a special event, like the state fair. Offer to come in one morning and change sheets, do laundry, or vacuum the floors. Take cookies, and offer to sit right beside the child with special needs while the mother and other children have a snack and special time together in the kitchen. Just 15 minutes alone with Mom or Dad can give a child a completely different perspective on her sibling with special needs and put a smile on her face.

Have a Little Fun

Aaron, being eight years old when Jay was born, took it upon himself to teach Jay all the "important" things in life. When I (Louise) came home one day, Aaron couldn't wait to show me what he had taught Jay. Since we all worked at creative play, even buying toys according to what they could do for Jay's cognitive skills or his gross and fine motor skills, I assumed Aaron had taught Jay something useful. Wrong!

"Okay, Mom, now watch this," Aaron said, and then he let out a loud burp. Just as I opened my mouth to reprimand him, I heard another burp from the sofa. Guess who! Jay! They laughed and laughed. Aaron was so pleased with himself.

Finally I got my wits about me and said, "This is what you taught him? How to burp on command?"

"Yeah," Aaron said. "Isn't it great?" The two of them collapsed into another fit of laughter.

I learned a big lesson that day: *Every kid deserves to be a kid.* Each waking moment does not have to be spent doing some therapy or other learning skill. Some of the greatest gifts God gives children with special needs are brothers and sisters. They fit together in His purpose and plan. They complement each other with their unique personalities, and they build relationships that are bonded in the deepest part of their souls. As you have seen in this chapter, their love and commitment to each other have no comparison.

Encouragement from Scripture

- "God has given each of you some special abilities; be sure to use them to help each other, passing on to others God's many kinds of blessings" (1 Peter 4:10, TLB).

- "I always thank God for you because of his grace given you in Christ Jesus" (1 Corinthians 1:4).

- "If you love someone you will be loyal to him no matter what the cost. You will always believe in him, always expect the best of him, and always stand your ground in defending him" (1 Corinthians 13:7, TLB).

- "God has given each of us the ability to do certain things well" (Romans 12:6, TLB).

- "But when the Holy Spirit controls our lives he will produce this kind of fruit in us: love, joy, peace, patience, kindness, goodness, faithfulness, gentleness and self-control" (Galatians 5:22, TLB).

- "And so I am giving a new commandment to you now—love each other just as much as I love you" (John 13:34, TLB).

- "Don't let anyone look down on you because you are young, but set an example for the believers in speech, in life, in love, in faith and in purity" (1 Timothy 4:12).

- "There has never been the slightest doubt in my mind that the God who started this great work in you would keep at it and bring it to a flourishing finish on the very day Jesus Christ appears" (Philippians 1:6, THE MESSAGE).

THE GIFT OF GRANDPARENTS

"He doesn't look like the other boys," Grandpa said as he viewed the blanketed bundle I (Louise) held in my arms. He was right. James Ryan, whom we called Jay-Jay, with his skinny legs, almost bald head, and tiny, up-slanted eyes, bore little resemblance to my other, chubby babies with their full heads of hair. But I knew the comment went far beyond looks. He couldn't accept Jay-Jay's mental handicap.

On subsequent visits, Pa-Pa, as the other children called him, ignored Jay-Jay. He picked him up once when it seemed to be expected for a family picture, but other than that he never touched him and looked upon him with something between pity and displeasure.

Then one day, a miracle began. We were at a family reunion, and Jay-Jay, being the outgoing little boy he was at three years old, walked over to his grandpa and crawled onto his lap. Pa-Pa was shocked, but what could he do in front of all those people? This was his grandson. How could they understand that he hardly knew Jay-Jay?

Jay-Jay took his grandpa's glasses out of his shirt pocket and placed them on his own face, upside down, precariously perched on his short, pudgy nose. He looked at Pa-Pa and giggled, making Pa-Pa laugh too—genuinely. Soon they were walking around the room, Jay-Jay leading Pa-Pa, a little smile on the older one's face.

Their next encounter came months later, when Pa-Pa decided to visit and Jay-Jay played the clown, making his grandpa laugh and pick him up and throw him into the air.

Then Pa-Pa turned to my husband and said, "Why, he's just like any other kid!"

We had tried to tell him, but Pa-Pa's preconceived ideas and fears of the disabled had kept him out of his grandson's life. But Jay-Jay would not let him remain in darkness. With his love and actions, he showed Pa-Pa and others that they were missing out on some of God's greatest blessings by not loving and caring for him.

After that day, a strong bond began to form. Pa-Pa found that Jay-Jay loved balloons and would have one waiting for him each time we went to visit—visits Pa-Pa now welcomed. Then he discovered that Jay-Jay was not only sweet but also ornery and loved pillow fights. So each visit would end up with pillows flying across the room. I never figured out which of the two enjoyed it most. Soon Pa-Pa began to telephone, supposedly to talk to my husband, who was now glowing in the new relationship between his father and his son. But Pa-Pa always insisted on speaking to his youngest grandson.

Jay-Jay can understand most of what's said to him. Yet because of a severe speech articulation disorder, he finds it difficult to form the words he wants to say, making communication difficult. Nevertheless, Pa-Pa always wanted to speak to him by phone, and Jay-Jay would laugh and talk in words that neither his dad nor I understood. Pa-Pa, on the other hand, swore he understood every word.

The phone chats became a weekly ritual. Every Saturday morning, Jay-Jay knew it was the day to talk to Pa-Pa. Since it was long distance, they took turns calling. But always, all excited, Jay-Jay would talk until we made him hang up.

Through the years, Jay, as he is called today, and Pa-Pa continued those weekly phone calls, along with exchanging letters and cards and going on fishing trips and trips to Wal-Mart together. They became "best buddies." Last year, when his beloved Pa-Pa died unexpectedly, Jay was given the American flag that had draped his casket. Jay cherishes the keepsake and tells us Pa-Pa is happy in heaven and has found a *big* Wal-Mart store there.

Praying a Blessing

Charles Stanley once said, "One of the purposes of grandparents is to pray blessings on their children's children." This is not only true but also biblical. A perfect example is when Joseph brought his sons to his father, Jacob, who laid hands on his grandsons' heads and pronounced blessings on them.

Today the tradition of placing hands on the child and bestowing a blessing is not widely practiced in the Christian community. But grandparents all over the world are still praying blessings on their children's children, and they're being blessed in return with a unique relationship that defies definition.

The grandparent-grandchild relationship can be one of the most strengthening ties in a child's life. He looks to his parents for love, guidance, shelter, protection, knowledge, and more, but he looks to his grandparents for a heritage—a blessing.

For the child with special needs, this relationship takes on an extra dimension. Many children with disabilities are already struggling with low self-esteem due to lack of acceptance by their peers. They need someone in their lives—besides their parents and siblings—to affirm their worth, spend time with them, take an interest in their activities, and share their thoughts and dreams. They need a grandparent to listen to their hearts, whether it be with words, sign language, or an unspoken communication with the eyes, mannerisms, or a smile.

Surely it's a special blessing to be the grandparent of a child who is sometimes seen as a mistake or a tragedy by the world, but who is a highly esteemed treasure to the almighty, holy God.

Let Us Help

When Gary and Barbara Lumpkin's son, Richey, was diagnosed with Duchenne muscular dystrophy at age four and a half, Barbara's parents called, insisting on visiting that very weekend.

"They barely got in the house before Mother said she was going to take Richey for a walk," says Barbara. "That left me alone with my dad. We sat and talked for a while, and then all of a sudden, Daddy scooted up to the edge of his chair and said, 'Barbara, we've come to offer our help.' I told him there was nothing they could do to help us."

Her father repeated his offer, and Barbara again declined, explaining they didn't need help. "Yes, you do," her father persisted. "I don't know what it is, but we've been praying about this, and I've been wrestling with the Lord. He told me to come to you and said there's some way we need to help you, but we don't know what it is."

Her parents offered to sell their home and move to the city where the Lumpkins lived, or to get an apartment and visit on weekends—a seven hour trip each way. They even offered to help financially. "We're here to help, but we don't know what you need," her father pleaded.

Barbara knew her parents to be dedicated Christians, having witnessed them fasting and praying about many decisions while she was growing up, and she was touched by this out-pouring of love. Still, she insisted there was nothing they could do.

Finally, her father broke down and cried, "You've got to let me help you, because I can't get any rest!"

Later that evening, Gary suggested a way Barbara's parents might help. "When I go on business trips, they can stay with Richey and keep him in his routine while you travel with me," he said. It was something she hadn't been able to do since Richey was born. Her parents readily embraced the idea, and for the next eight years, Richey's grandparents stayed with him four or five times a year—sometimes for a week at a time.

"It was almost like he had two sets of parents," said Barbara. "They developed a wonderful relationship with him, doing all the things I never had the patience to do, like 1,000-piece jig-saw puzzles, and Richey loved it. He was happy and laughed a lot."

Reflecting on that time, Barbara says, "When Richey was a baby, my parents thought he was cute and were glad we had him, but they didn't seem to take a special interest in him. After his diagnosis with muscular dystrophy, however, you couldn't keep them away. God really spoke to them, and they ministered to me in my depression, as well as to Richey. But I guess the greatest thing was the tremendous amount of love my father exhibited. It's like God gave him extra love just for Richey, and not a single negative thing happened in all those years. *Everything* was positive!"

Benjamin Scares Grandma

Sometimes a special-needs child will help to make a grand-parent's life exciting. When four-year-old Benjamin Graves's grandmother took him to his sister's soccer game, she hardly knew what she was in for. "Benjamin came and went, talking to other families on the team as he usually does," says his mother, Barbara.

When the game ended, Grandma gathered her things to go home and turned to get Benjamin, who has Down syndrome. But Benjamin had disappeared, "as only he can do," reports his mom. He was nowhere to be seen.

Grandma ran to Benjamin's sister, Mollyrose, and frantically exclaimed, "I can't find Benjamin anywhere!"

Mollyrose scanned the soccer field, which was totally fenced in except for the exit gate to the parking lot. "It's not likely that he got through there," she said. Then she looked more closely at the opposite side of the field, and there sat Benjamin, having a snack with the other team!

Heart of Love

When Adam Shepherd's grandmother died, his parents had no idea how he would react. Though they had lived miles away from her, they had spent a lot of time together, and she was very important to him.

Right before the funeral, 19-year-old Adam, who is develop-mentally delayed, went to his parents and asked if he could say something about his grandmother during the service. "We told him the program was already set," says his mother, Bonnie, "but Adam insisted." Though Bonnie had no idea what he would say, she realized this was important to him, so she asked the pastor if Adam could speak.

Much to everyone's surprise, Adam got up in front of the group and gave a beautiful eulogy of his love for his grandmother, telling how much she loved him and what a good grandma she had been.

"It was very simple language," says Bonnie, "but it was from such a heart of love that it touched everyone. Other people were unable to express their feelings, but here was this child who struggled with communication problems yet spoke spontaneously about wonderful times with his grandmother. It was a great time of healing and will always be a beautiful memory."

Tips for Grandparents

- *Educate yourself.* Read books, articles, and any other information available. Attend support meetings. Ask questions of the parents. When you understand the disability or illness, you can be comfortable around your grandchild. This takes a tremendous amount of stress off the parents, who otherwise have to explain every characteristic and behavior.

- *Learn your grandchild's routine.* If you live close enough to make weekly or monthly visits, learn your grandchild's routine. What does she eat? What time does he go to school? What medications is she taking? What's considered an emergency? This knowledge will help you enjoy your grandchild more, and you may even want to offer the parents a weekend away or to be available in case of an emergency. Invite your grandchild to spend a week of his summer vacation with you. Few children with special needs have this opportunity.

- *Learn how to communicate with your grandchild.* If he uses sign language, have the parents teach you some basic vocabulary, or take a class on your own. If the child uses gestures, mannerisms, eye movement, and so on to communicate, be a willing pupil, and learn how to translate. Communication helps build a strong bond with your grandchild.

- *Become involved.* Visit your grandchild as often as possible. If distance prevents it, send cards, letters, and recorded tapes, and call on the phone. Do something regularly that says, "I love you. I'm proud of you and glad that I'm your grandparent." Start this at an early age and it will help carry the child through adolescence. Children with special needs don't always have a lot of friends during adolescence and may experience a lot of rejection. An attentive grandparent can be a lifesaver. When you call, ask to speak to the child specifically. This makes her feel important and offsets the loneliness if other children in the family receive lots of calls from friends.

- *Be available but not judgmental to parents.* This might be tough, but sometimes parents just need to air their frustrations to someone. If they trust you enough to open their hearts and spill out raw emotions, don't stifle that communication by responding with trite clichés or judgmental statements. Don't worry about what you should say or do. Just love your child and grandchild, and be there when they need to cry about an injustice or brag about a milestone, however great or small.

- *Associate with other people who have special needs.* This is especially important if you aren't around your grandchild often. Volunteer at a school, Sunday school, or other organization that has children with special needs. This will help you remain comfortable around your own grandchild. Otherwise, there will always be a period of adjustment each time you visit, and you may never get to know him well.

- *Pray for your children and grandchildren.* Ask the parents for specific needs that you can pray about— doctor appointments, successful therapy, medications, seizures, good teachers and therapists, and more. Pray for good health, energy, and strength for everyone. Ask for a sweet disposition and friends for the child. And of course, pray for the child to come to a knowledge and acceptance of Jesus Christ as Savior. Have a special prayer time when the family visits. Pray for their safety on the way home, for a good week at school, or for a special event coming up. Let your children and grandchildren know you continually lift their names to our heavenly Father, and that you consider it a joy to do so.

Thirty Grandparents?

A couple of years ago, Valerie began taking her son, Brian, to the mall as part of his home-schooling routine. They worked on such life skills as using the escalator and elevator, counting money, and reading universal signs on restrooms. Brian's grandmother also went along and walked the mall with other senior citizens.

Soon Brian began greeting everyone with a friendly "Hi" each morning. As his grandmother picked up coffee in the food court before leaving the mall, Brian would mingle among the silver-haired men and women at the tables. Before long, he was sitting in the middle of the group and listening to stories from the "olden days."

Some of the seniors were in their eighties and nineties and doted on Brian as if he were their own grandson. Brian adopted all of them as his grandparents. Grandpa Dave is a retired pilot and brings him books on airplanes. Grandma Martha sometimes brings little gifts.

"There is no generation gap," says his mom. "They love Brian and treat him with respect." In fact, Brian has celebrated with so many seniors on their birthdays that he can hardly wait to celebrate his own birthday at the mall with all his adopted grandparents.

"I'm a senior citizen too," Brian tells his mom.

For Valerie, those relationships are an answer to prayer. Because Brian has such a wonderful relationship with his own grandparents, she often wondered how he would cope if anything happened to them. She began to pray that someone would be able to step in and become a substitute grandparent. What Brian got was *30* new grandmas and grandpas. And the best part? Brian is still blessed with his *own* loving grandparents. That makes *32* grandparents.

Four Hundred Cards

Adam Truman, 11 years old at the time of this writing, has lived with his grandparents, Wesley and Glenna, since he was 11 days old. "He can't walk or talk," says Glenna, "but he loves kids and music, laughs aloud, and makes eye contact. Adam is so precious to us. He is nothing but love!"

Living in the country, Glenna sometimes felt she and Adam were isolated. To counter that—and knowing how much Adam likes bright colors and pretty things—his grandmother wrote to a newspaper, explained Adam's situation, and asked if it would ask people to send birthday cards for Adam's sixth birthday.

"I thought he might get 50 at the most," says Glenna. What a surprise, then, when Adam ended up getting 400 cards! Some included prayers, letters, and pictures of other families who had children with special needs. "People wrote to tell us how special we were and that they were praying for us," Glenna continues. "It was a real surprise and so nice. I would hold the cards up for Adam to see, and he would smile at all the pretty pictures. We covered his walls with them so he could look at them while he was in bed."

Glenna still communicates with some of the families: "They send Adam cards for every occasion and sometimes include little gifts."

Five years after that outpouring of kindness, Glenna again wrote to the newspaper, requesting birthday cards for Adam. At the time of this writing, he has already received more than 200, and they're still coming in.

Tips for Parents

- *Involve and inform grandparents.* Let them know how they can help you. Do you need affirmation of their love and acceptance of your child? Tell them. Offer informative materials about your child's disabilities.

If they live close by, invite them over often so they can bond with their grandchild and learn his routine.

- *Be considerate of grandparents' time.* Though grandparents may enjoy baby-sitting occasionally, don't wear them out. They have other commitments and may still work full-time. Even if they're retired, their lives require daily routines, home maintenance, and difficult decisions about the future. Also, be aware of health limitations. Grandparents may not be able to lift a child who isn't ambulatory, but they can read stories, talk, work puzzles, listen to music, and have a snack with the child.

- *Keep communication open.* Talk about any problems. If you're concerned about a grandparent's health or about your own child's safety with a grandparent who is fragile, discuss it gently, with love. Also, discuss the problems you face with the school, doctors, friends, and so on, but always balance the conversation with the positive things you, as a parent, are experiencing.

- *Be aware that grandparents may be grieving.* In fact, they sometimes feel a double grief. They don't grieve just for the disabled child, but also for their own child as they see the hurt, disappointment, and struggles the parent is going through.

- *Allow grandparents to be grandparents.* If they want to pamper, dote, or brag, allow them to do so as long as it's within limits. If you have other children, recall whether they did the same with that child. If so, back off and let them "spoil" this child a little. If there really is too much or too little attention to the child with special needs, speak to the grandparents about your concern, but always in love.

- *Project positive expectations to grandparents.* Tell them what you expect from your child. No matter how severe the disability, every parent is always working toward a goal. Help the grandparents to overcome any negative attitude or a tendency to feel sorry for the child. Let them know that inside every *disabled* child is a *typical* child with the same love, hopes, dreams, and needs as other children.

Like Grandfather, Like Grandson

Jarvis Rolfe never had to worry about a ride to or from school or about whether someone would attend a special program he was in. His grandfather, Papa, was always there for his grandson who has Down syndrome.

"They were inseparable," says Jarvis's mom, Ruth. "Daddy was very active in the community, and he took Jarvis with him everywhere he went. Jarvis knows more people in the community than I do."

They even liked eating together, especially fried chicken. Some days after school, they would swing by Kentucky Fried Chicken and get a snack to tide them over until supper.

Jarvis's grandparents enjoyed his company so much that they never wanted him to go home. He enjoyed spending the night with them on several occasions. "They were just wrapped up in each other," says Ruth. "I had a wonderful support system."

She mentions a special picture she has of Jarvis and his Papa, who is now deceased, standing by the front porch. "They weren't doing anything in particular," she says. "But I look at that picture and remember all the fun they had 'just hanging out together.' That's what they enjoyed most—just being together!"

Practical Gems about Grandkids

Grandma Goes to the Movie

Rachel Richards is blessed to have three sets of grandparents. One grandma lives in Florida and takes her to Disney World when she and her sister visit for a week during the summer. She also spends occasional weekends with another set of grandparents. But the grandma who lives right in her own town can't keep Rachel, who has spina bifida, overnight. Due to a bone disorder, Grandma is unable to lift Rachel out of her wheelchair.

Wanting to spend extra time with her granddaughter, this grandma and Rachel's mom got creative and practical. On days when Rachel is out of school due to holidays, teacher's meetings, and so on and Mom has to work, Grandma takes her to a movie or on some other special outing. Rachel can wheel herself around without help, and a lightweight ramp gets her in and out of the van without problems.

Grandpa and Popcorn

One night as Grandpa was baby-sitting his granddaughter, Brittany Townsend, who has Rett syndrome, he came face to face with the impossible. Brittany couldn't communicate what she wanted. Grandpa couldn't guess, and both became upset. Brittany was throwing a tantrum by the time her mother came to pick her up. Since she's usually a happy child, especially with her grandparents, her mom knew something drastic had upset her.

Finally, they figured it out. On previous visits, Grandpa had always had a bowl of popcorn by his side. So this night, after quieting her with her favorite snack, Grandma and Grandpa put a large note on the refrigerator that reads: BRITTANY LOVES POPCORN! There have been no more problems.

Volunteer Grandmother

Jan Warren, a young lady with visual and hearing impairments and some autistic tendencies, moved across country with her mom and dad, leaving behind two brothers in college and seven special helpers at the church she loved. "We didn't know how she would react to a different school, different house, different church, different everything," said her father, Charlie. But Jan adjusted beautifully, thanks in large part to an older woman who volunteers in her class at school and whom all the kids think of as a grandmother. When Jan got up on Saturday after her first week in the new school, she signed "school," showing that she wanted to return. If only every classroom had a special grandma!

Granddad and Alzheimer's

Though Jay Jones doesn't know what Alzheimer's disease is, he knows his granddad is fragile, and he reaches out to him in love. When Jay first greets his grandparents, he zips by his grandmother and heads straight to his grandfather. He wraps his arms around Granddad, kisses his cheek, and pats him lovingly. Both grandfather and grandson look at Grandma and giggle as she feigns disappointment that she didn't get the first hug.

Jay can always coax a smile from his granddad, sometimes

the first of the day or even several days. At restaurants, Jay takes Granddad's arm and guides him to a chair, then pats the seat in a gesture to show him to sit down. When Granddad can't think of the words he needs to order his food and becomes frustrated, Jay, who has struggled with a speech artic-ulation disorder his whole life, pats his arm and says, "It's okay, Granddad." And it *is* okay. Granddad smiles genuinely, some-times laughs out loud, and lingers close to his affectionate, nurturing grandson.

Long-Distance Grandma

Because of the distance between their homes, Katie Young seldom saw her grandmother more than once a year. On one visit, Grandma hugged Katie, who has Rett syndrome, and said, "I know you don't remember me, but I'm your grandma, and I love you." Since Katie is unable to speak or respond nor-mally, her grandmother mistakenly thought she didn't know her.

Katie's mom, Dottie, who understands Katie's every sound and movement, realized differently, however. "Katie definitely knew her grandmother," she says. "I could tell by her smile and her actions that Katie was aware that this was a special person in her life—someone she loved, and someone who loved her." Dottie gently reminded Grandma of the ways that Katie expressed her love. Before the visit ended, Grandma understood and responded to Katie's love.

Adopted Grandparents

Bobby Walker is extremely compassionate and has an incred-ible ability to touch people's hearts. He has Tourette's syn-drome, but he visits a nursing home weekly with his mom, brother, and two sisters. On one visit, he met a lady named Ruby. The next time he was there, he ran over to her with a wide smile as if to say, "Remember me?"

The friendship blossomed, and on a subsequent visit, Bobby's mom was asked by a lady if all those children were hers. Before she could answer, Ruby spoke up and said, "Those three are hers, but that one is mine!" She pointed directly at Bobby, who had come to mean so much to her.

Encouragement from Scripture

- "But from everlasting to everlasting the Lord's love is with those who fear him, and his righteousness with their children's children" (Psalm 103:17).

- "It is possible to give away and become richer!" (Proverbs 11:24, TLB).

- "May you live to enjoy your grandchildren!" (Psalm 128:6, TLB).

- "How much better is wisdom than gold, and understanding than silver!" (Proverbs 16:16, TLB).

- "A good man leaves an inheritance for his children's children" (Proverbs 13:22).

- "I will pour out my Spirit on your offspring, and my blessing on your descendants" (Isaiah 44:3).

- "Children's children are a crown to the aged" (Proverbs 17:6).

CHAPTER 12

THE CHURCH AND FAMILIES WITH SPECIAL NEEDS

One of my (Louise's) sweetest memories is of when Jay was a toddler attending worship service. Every Sunday morning, he would run to our pastor after the service ended. The pastor would scoop him up in his arms and hold him while shaking hands with church members. I offered more than once to take Jay, but the pastor refused. In doing this, not only did he show his own love for Jay, but he also allowed the church members to meet and love Jay in a special way.

This helped Jay to feel as if he "belonged" to the whole church. What a marvelous blessing that has been in his life! Now 20 years old at the time I write this, Jay loves Jesus with all his heart and looks forward to church. Surely that pastor's love helped nurture Jay's sweet spirit and set an example for the church body to follow.

What if every pastor and church staff member modeled the same love and acceptance that our pastor gave Jay? Our churches would be a refuge for families with special needs who are seeking a place to worship.

Two Ministries Born

Donna Johnson and her husband, Alan, began with a vision for a Sunday school class that would meet the needs of their son, who has cerebral palsy, and other disabled children. Donna explains, "As a church, we have a scriptural responsibility to teach *all* children about Jesus so that one day, when they meet Him face to face, they can say, 'You're the one they told me about in Sunday school!'"

They presented their idea to the pastor and church board and received overwhelming support. But they also had another vision—respite care for families with special needs.

"It's great to *pray* for families with special needs," says Donna, "but having some time away is vital to their sanity and the overall health of the family." Within two weeks of starting their Sunday school class, Special Friends, they also began respite care. "I see this as evangelism," says Donna. "So many families are staying home from church. We need to be 'Jesus with skin on.' I just want to see all these people saved."

The respite care program has brought in more families than they can accommodate in one night. Since the church facility and workers can provide for a maximum of 25 to 30 children, and 60 families fill their list, they do an every-other-month rotation. And, of course, one of the greatest blessings is that many of these families are now attending church and Sunday school and growing in Christ.

Donna and Alan's vision continues to expand. The church is breaking ground for a new building, and they will have one of the largest rooms in the building to accommodate their growing ministry. They anticipate a bus ministry and a parent support group in their future.

"We want to see God's house full at Cathedral of Praise," say Donna and Alan. "Many of the empty chairs in our sanctuary are for families with disabled children. God is not going to fill every chair with able-bodied people who look like us, dress like us, talk like us, and act like us. God has called us to reach out to those in the disabled community, and we want to fulfill this calling until His return."

Tips from "Special Friends"

- Recruit "teaching teams." The size of each team will depend on the number of students. The best situation is to have one adult per child.

- Rotate. Special Friends uses four teams of six members each that rotate weekly, thereby requiring each person to volunteer only once a month.

- Greet the children at the door, even at the car if possible. Seat them at the front of the church, close to the music, and stay with them.

- Take students to the classroom when others leave for children's church.

- Hold regular training sessions for new volunteers.

Respite Care

Poodle skirts, pedal pushers, white T-shirts, and jeans are the fashion for both children and adults. Hula hoops and wheelchairs are in constant motion while a jukebox blasts out songs from the past. Colorful streamers decorate the youth chapel, seeming to float with the music. Oops, stop right there! Youth chapel? You mean this is part of a church? Yes. It's "Fabulous Fifties Night," and it's respite care for families of children with special needs.

For the next four hours, 25 kids will do the hokeypokey, compete in a bubble-gum-blowing contest, twirl a hula hoop somewhere on their bodies, and receive a ribbon for being "best of the best." And these kids will have so much fun that some won't even want to go home.

"That's when we know we've done a good job," says Donna Johnson, founder of the respite care. "In fact, some parents come back early rather than use the full four hours we give them, because they enjoy all the activity and being with other parents."

The group meets once a month, and each month there's a different theme. Once a year they do a western theme, complete with a wheelchair-accessible stagecoach. It's one of the kids' favorites. The children pan for "gold," then use the painted rocks to pay for their stagecoach fare. But no matter what the theme or disability, every child is included. And each month, some 35-plus volunteer workers do "one on one" as they guide wheelchairs or walkers, saddle little ones on their hips, or just try to keep up with a lively youngster.

"Not a single person is trained in special education," says Donna, who is also the mother of Eric, nine years old at the time of this writing. "We have two nurses present, which makes me feel comfortable, and about a dozen of us have had Red Cross and CPR training." The workers are all volunteers from the church.

You might wonder how they get 35 adults to commit to caring for disabled children one night a month. "It's short term," Donna explains. "They sign up for one night, and if they don't like it they don't have to come back. But once they get involved with the kids, they lose all their fears and you can't keep them away. The more they're around the children, the less they see the disability and the more they see the child."

One Person Is a Ministry!

Not every church will be able to provide a respite care program to its community. But every church can minister to the needs of its own members, even if only one person has such needs.

Shane Whitworth, a young man who is developmentally disabled, has gone to First Baptist Church in Madison, Alabama, all his life. In fact, his parents grew up in the same church. Shane has always been accepted and loved by the congregation, and as a child he was mainstreamed in a regular Sunday school classroom.

As an adult, however, his needs changed, and he was no longer comfortable in the class he was attending with younger students. His mother, Pat, mentioned the problem to their pastor and said she was going to start staying home with Shane during Sunday school. But within two weeks, Shane was provided a class of his own, with a husband-and-wife team as teachers.

"They are the sweetest, most gentle people you can imagine," says Pat, "and they've been so dedicated to teaching

Shane these past five years." Shane loves the class and doesn't mind at all that he's the only student. In fact, he seems to thrive on it, and he still enjoys plenty of socialization with people in the congregation.

Reverse Mainstreaming

If, on the other hand, a child or adult is unhappy in a class of one but still feels uncomfortable in a regular class, you can reverse the mainstreaming process. Have a couple of students from age-appropriate classes join the person with special needs in his class. One church did this when their children's class had only two students, and it worked beautifully. Both groups loved the interaction and learned how to accept each other and build new social skills.

When using reverse mainstreaming, it's important that the students from the regular class be excited and positive about joining the person with special needs. It should also be understood that the students are coming as *friends,* not helpers. Friendship implies equality, so if it's a children's class, make sure all the kids do the same activities. They don't have to do them in exactly the same way. For example, one may choose to write her own Bible verse, while another may have a teacher write it; then they can cut out their verses and glue them on the page themselves.

Volunteers from the regular classes could come for two to four consecutive Sundays, or you may want to use different volunteers every week. This gives more people the opportunity to be around students with special needs and see their particular learning styles and talents, but it doesn't offer a lot of time to build friendships. Each church and class must decide what's best for its students. No matter which you choose, it will be rewarding for everyone involved.

Heather's Helpers

As a young child, Heather Dittmer attended Northwest Bible Church in Dallas, Texas, with her family. Heather showed no signs of developmental delays until the age of three. Then suddenly, she wasn't talking like other children. By four and a half, Heather's disability became so great that her parents began to seek a diagnosis. More than a year later, she was diagnosed with muco poly saccharidosis, a rare disorder that affects only 1 in 100,000 people.

Heather's condition continued to deteriorate, and she began to lose skills she had already mastered. To permit her to continue in her Sunday school class, a couple of ladies became her personal escorts. They soon saw the need for more people and recruited other adults from their own Sunday school class. Eventually they ended up with *90* volunteers who became "Heather's Helpers." They helped her in the classroom with craft activities, such as gluing things. They escorted her to the bathroom and did anything necessary to allow Heather to continue participating in her Sunday school class and choir.

Eventually Heather lost so many of her abilities—even to the point of being back in diapers—that she could no longer attend class. Her parents switched off on Sundays, allowing one to go to church while the other stayed home. But Heather's Helpers stepped in again. People volunteered to care for her at home, allowing *both* parents to attend church together. One volunteer even stopped by McDonald's on the way to the house so she and Heather could have a picnic together.

When Heather was 12, her parents found it necessary to move her into a full-care facility because of the disease's ongoing progression. "It was a hard decision," says Bonnie, "but the

Lord showed us that this particular home was where she needed to be."

Bonnie says people still ask about Heather because they were either involved with or knew of Heather's Helpers. What a wonderful ministry to one family, and what an incredible witness of God's love through the church!

Melissa's Story

Unfortunately, the above examples are not the norm in the church today. Many churches don't offer programs to people with special needs, even when they have members who would benefit from them. The following story is just one example that's all too typical.

Ed and Cindy Hilton had attended and served in their church for several years before adopting Melissa, a beautiful little girl who was developmentally disabled. As a young child, she was mainstreamed in the Sunday school. Eventually, however, it became apparent that she needed a special program, since Melissa is visually and hearing impaired and has some autistic tendencies.

The children's minister tried in vain to find workers for Melissa. Finally, the church hired professional special education teachers, who were not of the same faith, to stay with Melissa. Though Ed and Cindy were grateful to the church for hiring the teachers, they could hardly believe that no one would volunteer to teach their daughter. After all, this was a large church, and Cindy had taught other people's children for 16 years.

Another problem was that Melissa and her teachers were not given a regular Sunday school room. They were relegated to a table in the front part of a storage room. Some Sundays, the room and table were so cluttered that it was almost impossible to clear a spot for Melissa to work. Again, her parents couldn't help but wonder why Melissa's needs were not a priority to the church.

The breaking point came one Sunday when neither of Melissa's teachers showed up. In the past, either Ed or Cindy had stayed home with Melissa if they knew a teacher was not available. However, this particular Sunday, the teachers failed to show without notice.

Cindy, who worked at the welcome desk, kept Melissa at her side that morning. Time after time, people asked why Melissa wasn't in Sunday school. Cindy explained to each person that her teacher hadn't shown up. Though most expressed a sympathetic "That's too bad," not one person offered to stay with Melissa.

The following week, Ed called a friend who was beginning a special education ministry in another church. Ed was assured that this other church could and *would* meet Melissa's needs. Ed and Cindy were skeptical but agreed to visit. When they did, they were pleased to see Melissa treated with love and respect. The teacher was compassionate and even volunteered to learn sign language, Melissa's only form of communication.

A month was all they needed to convince them that this was the church God intended for them. When they expressed a desire to be more involved in the church activities, they were assured Melissa's needs would be provided for, and they have not been disappointed.

Melissa now has seven volunteers who work with her at different times. But the best part is that she's happy and knows that people at the church love her. With that knowledge, Ed and Cindy now enjoy a much more worshipful experience. (*Adapted from Ed Hilton, "We Found a Caring Church,"* Special Education Today, *summer 1997.*)

When the Church Fails

It's estimated that 3 percent of the population has some mental disability. And Mark 16:15 gives us the responsibility, in our churches, to love, accept, and teach *all* people. Yet, according to Dr. James Dobson in a broadcast titled "Mothers of Handicapped Children," the church as a whole is not meeting the needs of the disabled. "There are exceptions," he says. "There are some churches that have programs for the retarded . . . the deaf . . . those who are in wheelchairs . . . but most churches do not. And people who have handicaps come to those churches and look around and see the absence of anybody else like themselves, and they feel a wall of misunderstanding and disapproval among those around them, and they don't come back. And I really feel that the Christian church is going to have to examine its values at this point, because there but for the grace of God go I or my child."

All of us should be asking these questions: Why aren't there more disabled people in church? Why aren't parents bringing their children with special needs? Why aren't group homes, intermediate-care facilities, and independent-living centers bringing their residents who are developmentally disabled? Better yet, why hasn't the church reached out to these families and individuals by offering special programs?

Perhaps the last question answers the preceding ones. If we in the church don't reach out and express a love for people with special needs, we can't expect them to attend. Parents of disabled children are not likely to visit a church without an invitation or knowledge of a program already in existence for their kids. They've been through too many disappointments to assume that anyone, even the church, will automatically accept their children. Many, like the Hiltons, have already been hurt by the church and are understandably skeptical.

One mother of a newborn child with special needs told us how a visit to her home from the pastor and a staff member was like a funeral call. Not only did they fail to encourage her and her husband, but they also failed to recognize the *worth* of their child.

Let's take our attitude toward disabled children and adults from Jesus. He touched people with leprosy and healed folks with all kinds of illness. He loved and valued every individual. God the Father does, too, and uses handicapped people in His plan. Moses, for example, was slow of speech, and Paul wrote of having a "thorn in the flesh." Throughout the Bible, we see God using what the world considered a disability or weakness for His glory.

Like the family mentioned above, I (Louise) sometimes encountered negative attitudes when our son Jay was born. Few people seemed to understand that I wasn't sitting around feel-

People with disabilities are God's best visual aids to demonstrate who He really is. His power shows up best in weakness. And who by the world's standards is weaker than the mentally or physically disabled? As the world watches, these people persevere. They live, love, trust and obey Him. Eventually the world is forced to say, "How great their God must be to inspire this kind of loyalty!"

Joni Eareckson Tada

Moody *magazine,*

October 1982

ing sorry for myself. I had a *beautiful* son and longed to have others voice the same opinion. Except for some special health problems, he was no different from any other child. But most failed to recognize this.

I remember a lady asking me to teach a class at a Thursday morning Friendship International meeting. With a background in foreign languages, I was excited and quickly agreed, provided she could find a baby-sitter for me. Jay's weak immune system didn't permit me to take him to a nursery. She said she was certain she could find someone in the church.

A few weeks later, she called to tell me that much to her surprise and embarrassment, she could find no one willing to come to my home and care for my son. Why? Was it fear, ignorance, lack of compassion, or all the above? I was disappointed but not really surprised. I had already noticed people's reluctance to be around me, even though I didn't know why.

I now realize that most people distance themselves from things they don't understand or are uncomfortable with rather than ask for information. But as a new mother, I wasn't looking for a textbook explanation. I was looking for a cup of coffee and companionship.

Another parent relates how she took her daughter and her friend to a special children's program at the church. Both girls were in wheelchairs. The usher directed them to a particular area, and she wheeled the girls in. But a man sitting nearby voiced his concern to the usher that he and his children might not be able to see above the wheelchairs. He even asked if any more of "those kind of people" were coming. What a sad example from the church body!

Many parents of disabled children go to church on Sunday morning with the desperate hope that this will be one place where their son or daughter will be accepted, having already been rejected by school classmates and neighborhood kids. When the church *doesn't* embrace these families, they're not likely to go down the street or around the corner and try another one. They leave with a sadness in their hearts that may eventually turn into anger and bitterness.

Oh, that we had the compassion of Jesus when He took one of those little children on His lap and said, "Whoever welcomes a little child like this in my name welcomes me" (Matthew 18:5)! What happens when the Body of Christ does not accept one of God's most precious creations—a child with special needs?

What Can the Church Do?

What are some ways the church can build a bridge to families with special needs and affirm the worth of their children?

- Be accessible! Offer plenty of handicapped parking and wheelchair cut-outs on curbs. Be sure doors and bathrooms are wide enough to accommodate a wheelchair. If you're planning a new facility, make every part of your building accessible, even the podium, choir loft, and baptistry—the areas most often overlooked. If your building is old and doesn't meet ADA (Americans with Disabilities Act) requirements, hire an architect to devise a plan for building a ramp, widening doorways, and providing accessible bathroom facilities.

- Offer extended care for children with special needs during the worship service. If a child's immune system is compromised, give the family its own private nursery in an empty Sunday school room, complete with worker. Many parents would like to be involved in different aspects of ministry during worship—choir, special music, orchestra, drama, ushering, and so on. By offering a place for all children to be loved, cared for, and taught about Jesus, both the parents and the caregivers are using the special gifts God gave them to bless the Body of Christ.

- Offer alternatives for the visually impaired—large-print bulletins and newsletters, better lighting, well-marked sidewalks, and a printed text of the information projected onto overhead screens.

- Draw *near to,* not *away from,* these families. Acknowledge the worth of their children. One mom says, "I wish someone would have wrapped her arms around me when my son was born and said, 'God made your child, and he will touch a lot of lives.' That would have given me hope."

- Include the child who is disabled in *all* activities, not just Sunday school. If you offer children's choirs, mission activities, vacation Bible school, or summer programs, make sure the child with special needs has the chance to be a part of them as well. One church had a group of disabled children perform a Christmas play based on *The Crippled Lamb,* by Max Lucado. Most of the children couldn't walk or talk, but they had beautiful, airy wings coming out from their wheelchairs.

- Offer social activities for a group of adults who are

developmentally disabled. Have a pizza party or ice cream social, just as you would for a regular singles class. If you have only one or two special-needs adults, include them in the singles program.

- Invite children, teens, and adults to sing in age-appropriate choirs. One of the greatest joys of deveopmentally disabled people is singing about Jesus. They may not sing in perfect pitch, but then, the only perfect choir is in heaven.

- Treat the family with special needs like a typical family. Realize that the members have careers, talents, interests, and hobbies, and that the family probably has children besides the one with special needs. Carole Scott says, "I have hobbies, two other children, a grandchild, and another on the way. Yet people don't talk to me about anything except Ben [her son with special needs]."

- Never grow tired of listening to or praying for the concerns of the family with special needs. Each stage of development brings new challenges and new pain. Listen lovingly, with a nonjudgmental attitude. Remember, their problems are ongoing. While their friends' lives usually progress predictably, theirs will be forever unique.

- Develop a buddy system for adults with disabilities, who may not have family or friends to sit with in the church service. Be a friend, but understand the commitment that goes with it. If you invite someone to sit with you during worship, expect him to sit with you the following Sunday as well. Disabled adults are very loyal, and the reward of their friendship will be worth the effort you put into it. You might also call at your friend's group home or facility once or twice a month, or even invite him out for a hamburger on occasion.

- Allow people with special needs to minister to the church body. When God gave gifts, He didn't skip the disabled. Discover their talents, and then find a place for them to serve, whether it's in singing, directing traffic, taking the offering, or praying. Enrich your church by allowing these faithful members to minister to your congregation.

- Offer sign language for the hearing impaired. In fact, offer classes in sign so that Bible study teachers and others can learn to communicate with those who are nonverbal.

- Begin a parent support group. Not only will this help parents in the church, but it could also be an outreach to the community.

- Provide respite care for parents, even if it's only once a month. Many couples can't get out together any other way. Even when regular child care is provided for church social functions, many times nothing is provided for the child with special needs.

- Recruit volunteers to go to the home and stay with a medically fragile or total-care child at least one Sunday morning a month so both parents can attend church together. Also offer the couple an evening away from home. One mom says, "The church needs to be aware that if they can learn the child's routine and give parents some relief, they would possibly be saving a marriage as well as the family." Some parents have children in residential facilities because of medical needs. These parents need to know that the church hasn't forgotten them, either. Pray for the family, send cards to the children regularly, and accompany the parents on visits to their children's homes.

• Ask the families if there's anything they need. Some families need practical things, like a ramp built for a wheelchair.

Realize that most families will not *ask* for help but will accept it if offered. The church can be a great blessing to them. A family in Kansas received so much love and support from their church that the parents are certain the church would take care of their daughter with special needs should anything happen to either of them. Now, that's a testimony!

God's Handiwork

While speaking candidly about loving others in a message titled "What About My Neighbor's Neighbor?" Chuck Swindoll related the story of a couple in his church who had two developmentally disabled adult children. One day their mother, Gloria Hawley, slipped the following paraphrase of Jesus' words from Matthew 25:35-40 into his hand:

"'I was afflicted with cerebral palsy, and you listened to my faltering speech and gently held my flailing hands. I was born a Down syndrome child, and you welcomed me into your church. I was retarded, and your love reached out to me.'

"And the people said, 'Lord when did we see You with cerebral palsy and listen to You? And when were You born with Down syndrome or retarded?'

"And He said, 'Ah, in that you did it unto the least of these My people, you did it unto Me.'"

How One Church Progressed

Twelve years ago, Henderson Hills Baptist Church in Edmond, Oklahoma, began a ministry to people with special needs with only one child. The next year, attendance had grown to just two students. But the workers took heart, saying they were the only department in the church that had doubled its size in one year! The following year, residents from the group homes in the area heard of the ministry and began to attend, ushering in a new program for adults with developmental disabilities. More parents learned of the children's program as well, and that Sunday school class grew to five.

Each year, the program grew in some way. One year a bus ministry was added, then a vacation Bible school for children. A "Special Friends" ministry was started in which developmentally disabled adults were invited to sit with a family in the worship service.

From the beginning, one Sunday out of the year was designated as "Special Ministry Day." On this day, the congregation has the opportunity to hear the students sing songs, recite Bible verses, and participate in puppet skits. Teachers and parents of children with special needs also give testimonies of how God has blessed them.

Every year in December, the students dress up in their Sunday best for a sit-down Christmas banquet in which adults and youth from the church lovingly serve them a several-course meal. The students are also treated to special entertainment, a gift bag filled with goodies, and a professional photograph of themselves taken beside the Christmas tree. It's an exciting day for them, and they usually end it by singing Christmas carols.

Today the Henderson Hills special ministries department has an enrollment of approximately 60 individuals in Sunday school, not including those who are mainstreamed. The students range in age from infants in the nursery to a gentleman nearing 70. An extended session for children who aren't able to attend the worship service with their parents is also provided.

The newest ministry is a choir called Joyful Sound, complete with matching T-shirts. The group has already performed for the church congregation and at a Sunday school training seminar for special-education workers. Other areas of the ministry are a parent support group and a special ministries team that facilitates the above programs and reaches out to new families in the community. The team also holds training sessions for other churches wanting to start their own ministry.

The way hasn't always been smooth and easy for the workers, but it has been worth the effort. Some programs worked for a while and then went by the wayside; others took years to develop. And, of course, there's always room for more volunteers and teachers. There are still areas the team hopes to develop, too, such as a program on Wednesday night for children, more social activities for the adult members, respite care for parents, and training sessions for *all* Sunday school workers. But the important thing is that the ministry is progressing and families are being served.

Many of the adults in the program are involved in a discipleship course, and several have made commitments to Jesus

Christ. When asked what impressed her most about the students, one teacher replied, "Their spirit of worship, their open love and deep prayer life."

If your church has yet to start ministering to people with special needs, ask God to direct you in how you can minister to this population. See the materials in the resource section (e.g., the listing for Friendship Foundation/Friendship Ministries) that can help you get started. Don't worry about starting small. Whether you serve 1 or 100, it's a ministry, and you and your whole congregation will be blessed with every step you take.

Lighter Side

Preston, an active eight-year-old with Down syndrome, decided to join his sister, who was sitting with the youth in another section of the sanctuary. The worship service was almost over, and without his mother's knowledge, his sister was encouraging him to join them.

Before Mom realized it, Preston had left his seat and was headed toward the youth section. Once there, he immediately gave his sister a big hug, then hugged her friend beside her. But instead of next sitting down, he continued along the row, hugging people. Then he went right on to the next row and the next. Finally, 15 rows and 100 people later, he had given *every* young person a big hug.

His parents were just thankful the pastor was only giving announcements at the time!

Encouragement from Scripture

- "Now you are the body of Christ, and each one of you is a part of it" (1 Corinthians 12:27).

- "How great is the love the Father has lavished on us, that we should be called children of God!" (1 John 3:1).

- "Let us fix our eyes on Jesus, the author and perfecter of our faith" (Hebrews 12:2).

- "And then he told them, 'You are to go into all the world and preach the Good News to everyone, everywhere'" (Mark 16:15, TLB).

- "The Holy Spirit displays God's power through each of us as a means of helping the entire church" (1 Corinthians 12:7, TLB).

- "For the Kingdom of God belongs to men who have hearts as trusting as these little children's. And anyone who doesn't have their kind of faith will never get within the Kingdom's gates" (Luke 18:17, TLB).

(Most people with developmental disabilities have this kind of faith. It doesn't mean they can't understand any better than a child. On the contrary, it means they have a special love and longing for Jesus that can be found only in the pure of heart.)

- "'Everyone who calls on the name of the Lord will be saved.' How, then, can they call on the one they have not believed in? And how can they believe in the one of whom they have not heard? And how can they hear without someone preaching to them? And how can they preach unless they are sent? As it is written, 'How beautiful are the feet of those who bring good news!'" (Romans 10:13-15).

CHAPTER 13

WHEN I GROW UP: ADULTS WITH SPECIAL NEEDS

What do you want to be when you grow up?

"I want to be a doctor or teach math on a computer," says Jarrod, who has cerebral palsy.

Rachel, who was born with spina bifida, wants to be a school teacher.

"I want to own a car wash when I grow up," says Brian.

"A preacher," says Jay.

And Richey wants to be the manager of a basketball team.

It's a simple question that we ask children we don't even know, yet sometimes we fail to ask it of children and young people with special needs. We need to remember that they have hopes, dreams, and goals just like everyone else.

When other children say they want to be a nurse, school teacher, firefighter, truck driver, or dancer, we don't squelch their enthusiasm but rather encourage their dreams and nurture their talents. We need to do the same for children with special needs. True, some of their aspirations may not be possible, but *having* dreams is a healthy thing.

If we don't step on those dreams, they just might come true. Look at Heather Whitestone, who became the first disabled Miss America in the history of the pageant. Jean Driscoll earned the Women's Sports Foundation's Amateur Sportswoman of the Year Award in 1991 when she won the Boston Marathon for the second time with her Day-Glo® yellow racing chair.

Miss America

Heather Whitestone lost 95 percent of her hearing when she was 18 months old due to an infection. The medicine prescribed saved her life but robbed her of most of her hearing. Determined that her daughter would speak nonetheless, Heather's mother, Daphne, enrolled her at the Dorren Pollack Clinic in Denver, which advocates *ocoupedics*—learning to *listen* and speak rather than use sign language. The staff explained that Heather could always learn to sign later, but she wouldn't always have the ability to learn to speak.

In addition to speech and hearing therapy, her mother enrolled Heather in a dance class. And even though she was unable to hear or feel the music, she fell in love with ballet. She learned to memorize the counts, then dance to the music God has placed in her heart. As Miss America 1995, Heather opened eyes and ears to the needs of the disabled, and she has proved that dreams can come true for those with special needs.

Sportswoman of the Year

Jean Driscoll was born with spina bifida, club feet, and a cleft palate. She went through multiple surgeries to correct various problems. Today, as a wheelchair athlete, she sets a grueling pace for herself, training five hours a day, six days a week. Her efforts have paid off. At the time of this writing, she has won the Boston Marathon seven times and most recently took home a silver medal in the 800 meter race at the Olympics in Atlanta. Jean followed that with two gold medals, one silver, and one bronze in the Paralympics, where 4,000 athletes with disabilities compete.

Jean readily admits she's a competitor and doesn't keep up her vigorous training schedule strictly to be courageous or inspirational. She likes to win! But after giving her life to Christ, she acknowledges that His strength is what allows her to perform. She now wants Him to get the glory, claiming the victories are His, not hers.

TV Star

Christopher Burke is a young man with Down syndrome. His name became well known when he starred in the TV series *Life Goes On.* He became a positive role model for many teenagers with special needs, including my (Louise's) son Jay.

No, Jay has no desire to become an actor, but he loved watching "Corky" on TV. He emulated him in many ways. When Corky was happy, Jay was happy. When Corky was mistreated, Jay was sad. And when Corky got a leather jacket, Jay wanted one, too! He identified with Corky and his daily struggle for acceptance, because he wanted the same thing for himself.

Teacher of the Year

"I wanted to be a teacher as early as third or fourth grade because teachers are bright, creative, and innovative people," says Richard Ruffalo, the 1995 outstanding teacher of the year and outstanding athletic coach of the year in the Walt Disney/McDonald's American Teacher Awards competition. "I love people, and I always wanted to be a significant someone in others' lives." Though he's already a significant person to his wife, Dianne, and daughter, Sara, teaching also helps him achieve that goal.

Rich Ruffalo is blind, having lost his sight more than a decade ago, at the age of 32. "I may not be able to see my students, but I can identity all of them," he says. He wants to bring out his students' hidden talents and make champions of them.

If anyone knows how to build a champion, it would be Rich Ruffalo, who spends hours listening to and memorizing tapes of textbooks and also competes in many athletic events. He's a member of the U.S. disabled sports team, has won 19 national titles, and has set 15 national records in track and field while competing against other physically challenged athletes. He has also won 11 masters championships against able-bodied competitors in shot put, javelin, discus, and power lifting. Further, he has picked up an impressive number of medals at the International Paralympics and the regular Olympics.

The one thing greater than Rich's love for sports is his passion for the Lord. "If I replace me, myself, and I with the Father, the Son, and the Holy Spirit, wonderful things happen," he reports. And wonderful things happen to the kids he teaches and coaches.

"I love coaching for the same reasons I love teaching," says

Rich. "It's an opportunity to give of myself, to show random acts of kindness, and to help kids win invisible gold medals of character." (*Adapted from* Teachers in Focus, *May/June 1996, pp. 8-12.*)

Seeker of God's Heart

In 1967, a diving accident left Joni Eareckson Tada a quadriplegic, paralyzed from the shoulders down. A teenager and just out of high school, Joni was devastated by the severity of her injury. Hopes and dreams were shattered. Her injury left her totally dependent on others. Someone else had to get her out of bed, dress her, feed her, brush her teeth, and comb her hair. The future seemed to hold little promise. But Joni still held a dream—to be all that God intended her to be.

Today, after three decades in a wheelchair, Joni is founder and president of JAF Ministries (Joni and Friends), an organization that conducts Christian outreach in the disabled community. A popular JAF ministry is their family retreats, which are designed around the unique needs of families who have a member with disabilities. (See the resource section for more information.) Another ministry is Wheels for the World, which restores and distributes thousands of used wheelchairs annually to disabled people in other countries. The ministry actually restores lives by meeting people's physical needs while telling them about Jesus Christ.

Joni has won scores of awards and honors and is known internationally not just for her work with the disabled, but also as an inspirational speaker, artist (she holds the brush in her mouth), author, and singer. She has spoken at Billy Graham crusades, has her own radio program, and is a disability advocate, always promoting a Christian perspective on issues that affect people with disabilities.

Married to Ken Tada for 15 years at the time of this writing, Joni still has to depend on others for her personal needs. But she continually praises and glorifies God through her writing, speaking, and painting. Her dream is still that God would use her life for His glory, and that others might come to know salvation through Jesus Christ.

Fulfilling Dreams

Most of us won't be the next Miss America or a famous actor, athlete, or speaker, but we all have potential. And we, as parents, teachers, pastors, doctors, or friends, are responsible for helping young people and adults with special needs to develop their full potential.

If the disabled person is just leaving high school, he may have several options available. He may want to pursue college, attend a vocational school, or work at a sheltered workshop or a job in the community. Your state vocational rehabilitation agency may be of assistance, especially if he needs special training for a job. A counselor can help assess his interests, potential, and limitations and even help obtain such auxiliary aids and services as interpreters or speech devices necessary for functioning in a work environment. Some states begin transitioning students while they're still in high school; others wait until graduation. Call your state organization.

Whether working with an agency or not, whether we're parents or not, we all need to help our special-needs adults become as independent as possible and encourage them to fulfill their potential. Maybe you know a disabled adult who wants to sack groceries or work in a restaurant or movie theater. Foster that dream! Perhaps you know one who has a real knack for fixing cars and wants to work in a garage. Help her look into it. Somebody will probably offer the opportunity. Do you know someone who has a sweet, gentle spirit and is excellent with preschoolers? Contact a day-care center or even a church nursery. Do what it takes to make life more than an existence for adults with special needs.

Now, some of you are probably wondering what planet we live on. Perhaps your child is totally dependent and requires full-time care. He seems to have no choices, no alternatives. When someone talks about independent or supported living, you leave the room. Why should you subject yourself to the torment? Your child will never even see the inside of a group home, for heaven's sake! Your adult child may live at home, in an intermediate-care facility, or even at a full-care nursing home or hospital.

Nonetheless, this chapter is still for you, because *every* person has a dream and a gift from God. Every person is valuable to God and has a unique talent that will further His kingdom. It may be a special smile, a twinkle in the eyes, or a kindred spirit that just "connects" with another person. Loving hearts don't always communicate with spoken words. Whatever your adult child's ability or disability, God *can* and *will* use it for His glory!

The Warmth of a Touch

Nothing is easy for Doug Cox unless it's his contagious smile. On second thought, even the smile probably comes with effort. Doug was born with cerebral palsy, and at the time his parents were given a bleak prognosis.

"I consider everything he does a miracle," says his mother, Nova, "because we were told he would never do anything. If he sits up or rolls over, I consider it a miracle. Everything he does is amazing to me!"

Now 34 years old at the time of this writing, Doug has lived at an intermediate-care facility for the past six years. Before that, he lived at home. The facility is small and close to home, so his parents are able to visit him every weekend.

Doug loves interaction with people; he likes being with someone all the time. He doesn't communicate with speech, however. "Doug communicates with his eyes, his smile, facial expressions, and laughter," says his mom, who knows him from top to toe. She has watched not only Doug's expressions through these 34 years, but also the actions of others.

To help people become comfortable with Doug, his parents taught him to shake hands. Living on a ranch and raising horses, the family often attended horse shows. Doug always went along, but people didn't know how to respond to him. To help, one of his parents would say, "Doug, shake hands with Mr. Smith." Doug would put out his hand, and the tension broke when the hands clasped.

"I believe it's the touch," says Nova. "The warmth of touch is a sign of acceptance. Doug automatically accepted them; now they were accepting him. But parents have to lead the way, even for other children in the home. You must demonstrate love and acceptance of your child, and then others will usually do the same."

She acknowledges, however, that there are still times when your child will not be accepted. "You learn to read people by the way they act," she says. "When people shy away from Doug, I think, *Oh, they have so much to learn.* You see, the disabled person has no problem interacting with them. They're the ones with the problem."

Nova's advice for parents is simple: "Accept your child, love him, and get on with life. Never feel sorry for the person with the handicap. He's learning and doing the best he can. What more could you expect?"

She quickly adds that without acceptance, a disabled person—like anyone else—feels uncomfortable. Even an argument between his mom and dad can make the special-needs person uncomfortable if the disagreement involves him. Nova also believes a child's personality develops out of the way he's accepted.

"Doug knows people by their personality," says Nova. "He knows them by their laughter and the attention they give him." She recalls a college student who used to do therapy with Doug. "They would get on the trampoline, and Doug would laugh and laugh as the young man bounced him up and down. They both just had a ball."

The desire for that type of interaction has kept Nova searching for unique opportunities for Doug and others who are severely disabled. She was co-founder and executive director of the local ARC for more than 20 years.

"I'm continually dreaming," she says. "I think of concerts, swimming, university programs—anything that will keep them interacting and doing!"

Nova also insists that Doug be taken to church regularly. He attends a class for adults with special needs and seldom misses a Sunday. He especially loves the music.

Even though Doug's skills are extremely limited, you'll find no self-pity in his mom. "Every child with special needs is an act of God," she says. "It's up to us to accept this child and do something to make his life better and happier. It will change the way we think and live forever."

Lee Ann's Apartment

"I've got my own apartment!" Lee Ann's voice practically leaped through the phone line. "And guess what?" she said, bursting with excitement. "Today I got my first bill!"

I (Louise) couldn't contain my laughter. "Lee Ann," I said, "you're the only person I know who is excited about getting a *bill* in the mail." But for Lee Ann, who has Down syndrome and was 44 years old at the time of our conversation, this was a dream come true.

"There was nothing available for her in the educational system," says her mother, Pat, who knew that schools were allotted funds for educating children with disabilities but met one closed door after another when she tried to enroll Lee Ann. Pat educated Lee Ann the best she could at home. Then, when Lee Ann was 12 years old, Pat began driving her to a state school for a half-day program.

A year and a half later, Lee Ann asked to live at the school. "That was a hard decision for her dad and me," says Pat. "But Lee Ann felt *different* because the other children lived at the residential facility. She also missed the social interaction of her friends."

Lee Ann was allowed to live at the school but still came home every weekend and holiday. After graduating at 18, she returned home, where she worked at a day-care center and volunteered her time helping students train for Special Olympics. But she longed for more independence.

While visiting her brother's church one Sunday, Lee Ann and her mom met a lady who was starting a group home for young women and invited Lee Ann to spend a week. Lee Ann agreed. After only two days, she called home to plead, "Oh, Mother, I love it here! Do I have to come home?" She eventually spent nine years at the group home, but she also held a goal of one day living independently.

"I wanted to do things on my own," says Lee Ann now, "and I'm doing them. I buy my own groceries, pay my own bills, and have my friends over to swim or whatever." Lee Ann also works at a work center and a restaurant.

"The group home mom picks me up for church," says Lee Ann, who is an extremely dedicated member. When asked to describe herself, she says, "I'm a friendly person, secretary of my Sunday school class, and I love to sing about the Lord. I love my church. I would do anything for my church!"

Having spent a lifetime going to church and always witnessing for Jesus, Lee Ann led her father to Christ only days before he died. "I was at work," says Pat, "but when I got home, Lee Ann said, 'I told Daddy about Jesus, and he asked Jesus into his life.'"

"I loved my daddy and still miss him," Lee Ann says. "I love my mom dearly. If anything happened to her, I would be lost. She's seen my apartment and told me how proud she is of me." Lee Ann pauses, then adds enthusiastically, "I'm proud of myself and what I'm doing!"

And Pat says of her independent daughter, "Lee Ann has always been a special blessing to our whole family and is proof that God makes no mistakes."

Building a Group Home

Gene and Joy Nabi are the parents of five children. Their middle son, Scott, has a genetic disorder that resulted in mental retardation. Scott is now 35 years old at the time of this writing and enjoys living in a group home not far from his parents. But the road to independence was not easy for Scott or his parents.

"While growing up, Scott had a stormy personality," says Joy. "Looking back, I think we may have expected too much of him. Being in the middle of five kids, he was raised like our other children. I'm not saying this is the wrong thing to do, because I think you should treat your child as normally as possible, within the range of his disability. But you also need to understand he won't always do things on the same scale. Sometimes I think we should have made more allowances for Scott—given him a longer time frame to accomplish everyday routines."

Joy also encourages parents to explore respite care. Scott was never one to enjoy vacations since he didn't like traveling and eating out. It made it hard on both Scott and the family. Finally, Joy took advantage of a respite service in which a couple took Scott into their home for two weeks. Joy and Gene could travel, knowing Scott was well cared for and much happier than if he were on the road with them.

When he became an adult, they felt certain that a group home with a Christian atmosphere would greatly benefit him. So they began to look for a proper facility. All too many parents of adult children with special needs understand the difficulty of this situation. Not finding what they wanted, however, the Nabis finally took things into their own hands. They organized a group of people—parents, attorney, grandparents, and anyone interested—and began a nonprofit organization. Their dream was to *build* a group home with a Christian atmosphere for developmentally disabled adults.

They started a campaign for donations with a newsletter called *The Encourager*, encouraging people to support them in their efforts. Eventually, they asked the Tennessee Baptist Convention to become involved.

The Convention agreed to take over a group home provided it was debt free. It took the group three years to raise enough money for the first group home. Then five years later, it opened a second facility. True to its word, the Tennessee

Baptist Convention now operates the facilities.

At the age of 29, Scott moved into the group home, not at all certain this was what he wanted. But Gene and Joy were enthusiastic, feeling the need for a home for Scott if anything should happen to them.

"We believe any change for an adult child with special needs should be made while the parents are still around," says Joy. "He can still come home to a family, which Scott does once a month, but he's also building a family at his group home. If parents wait until they're in the hospital—or even worse, if they die—the child is completely devastated. He has lost everything!"

Scott has now been at the group home for six years at the time this is being written, and he thrives on the routine. Though he enjoys going to see his parents, he's always eager to get back to his *other* home.

"He's like a different person," says Joy. "He's happy, loving, and affectionate. I never thought he would be this way. He also has a great spiritual depth. He prays and talks a lot about God and what would please Him."

Gene and Joy have set up a trust fund to make sure Scott will always be able to live in his group home, no matter what happens to them. "As a parent, you always wonder who will take care of your child and love him when you're gone," says Joy. "If anything happened to Gene or me, I know Scott would miss us terribly and grieve. But he would still have a home!" That knowledge gives the Nabis great peace.

Tips for Parents of Adults with Special Needs

- *Allow your adult child to be as independent as possible.* If she lives at home, give her as much responsibility as she's able to handle. But by the same token, don't frustrate her by expecting her to exceed her capabilities. Also, give her the freedom to develop her unique personality.

- *Keep a routine.* Most developmentally disabled people thrive on routine. They need to know what to expect each day. Ideally, the child will be able to attend a school or work program. Many communities have sheltered workshops. If the child must stay at home for medical reasons, bring someone into the home to work with him so he can remain productive and feel good about himself.

- *Help your child develop a deep spiritual life.* Pray aloud with her, and talk often about how much Jesus loves her. Give her a Bible, and read it together. Take her to church regularly, and give her tapes of Christian music, along with a tape player. If she lives in a residential facility, insist that she be taken to church on Sundays.

- *Dismiss negative thinking.* Never look back and say, "If only I had done this differently, or if I hadn't done that." Those are destructive thoughts. You did the best you could with what was available for your child at the time. You can't expect more, even of yourself.

- *Remember that your child is unique and uniquely gifted.* What works for one person may not work for another. You know your child better than anyone else. When making decisions concerning his future, go with your own instincts. Do what you believe is best for his particular situation, keeping in mind the way God has gifted him.

- *Take care of yourself.* When you feel well physically, mentally, emotionally, and spiritually, you can cope with things much better. Keep yourself involved with other people, and pursue some hobbies or interests outside the needs of your child. If you're the major caregiver for your disabled child, try to get away for a day, an evening, or even a weekend. It gives you and your child a much-needed break.

- *Go to support meetings for parents with adult children.* Talk candidly about your feelings. Maybe you're feeling overwhelmed with the long-term responsibility, or perhaps you need information about group homes or total-care facilities. There's no guarantee you'll be able to get that information immediately, but neither will the other parents judge you for what you're feeling, and that alone is worth the visit. If you're looking at placement, no one can help you as much as a parent who has been where you are. Some facilities have their own support groups for parents (or have permission to give you another parent's phone number).

- *Seek counseling if you're dealing with a difficult situation.* If possible, find a counselor who has worked with disabled individuals. That will allow you to focus on the problem at hand rather than feeling the need to explain your unique lifestyle.

- *Communicate with your child.* Many disabled adults want to be independent. They want a job and their own apartment or a group home. But they may be concerned about how *you* will cope without them. Keep the lines of communication open.

- *Keep your child involved in social activities.* Here are some suggestions for places to go: church and church-related activities; lunch or dinner at a favorite restaurant; a movie; miniature golf; and bowling (bumper guards and ramps are available for those who need them). And don't forget about the wide range of activities available through Special Olympics—sports, music, and art. Also, many regular sports have teams especially for disabled individuals.

- *Find a special friend for your disabled child.* Try to find a special person with whom your child can spend time. It may be another disabled adult, a senior adult, a teenager, or even a relative. She will enjoy having someone besides a parent involved in her life.

- *Do things as a family.* If your child lives at home, you have many opportunities to do things together. If not, plan special activities for weekends when your child is at home. Go on picnics; rent videos; work on puzzles; listen to music; read a book together; play simple board or computer games (special adaptive switches can be installed for those who can't manipulate the keyboard or mouse). Take a short trip to a lake or scenic area, and let your child draw, paint, or take pictures with a Polaroid camera. Choose *any* activity that suits your child, your family, and your lifestyle, and have some fun together!

What Handicap?

Michael Woolsey, a young man with Down syndrome, lives at home with his parents and wouldn't have it any other way. His parents, Robert and Joanne, are certain Michael will let them know if and when he wants to move into more independent living. "We've talked about it, and we always take our cue from Michael," says Joanne. That has worked in most situations, including the time he decided he wanted to learn to drive.

"We were a little apprehensive about him driving and wondered if this was going to be the first time we had to tell him he couldn't do something," says Joanne. "We had never told him he was unable to do anything because of his disability." Since Michael was 16 at the time, they followed the normal procedure and contacted the driver's education instructor. He gave Michael a book and told him he had to read it and pass a written test, and then he could learn to drive. Though Michael is literate, reading is not one of his favorite pastimes. "He just decided it was too much trouble," says his mom, "and we never heard any more about it."

But Michael is no stranger to work. When he was 18, he finished high school and began working mornings as a teacher's aide for preschool children with special needs. He spent his afternoons working with a grounds crew on the campus of a private school. Now 37 at the time of this writing, he still works his afternoon job at the school, volunteers his mornings as a teacher's aide in a preschool, and swims 20 laps in a pool per day.

Michael did take a recent summer off from his volunteer job, however. "He had never before had a good vacation," reports Joanne. "But he doesn't even think about taking a vacation from his landscaping work because he gets a paycheck."

Michael has lots of success stories, including a speech he gave to a group of adults who were studying to become special education teachers. "Michael had given a speech and slide presentation about his family, his life, and his work to a group of parents to fulfill one of the requirements for his Eagle Scout badge," says Joanne. "This teacher heard about it and asked him to make the same presentation to his college students."

During the question-and-answer period following the presentation, one woman stood and asked him how he managed his handicap. Michael quickly replied, "What handicap?"

His parents believe that comment is a perfect description of Michael. "His scout leader always told him that a handicap is just in your mind," Joanne reports. "If you don't think you have one, you don't. We feel the same way."

Late-Night Pizza

If you want conversation, Rhonda Thompson is a great person to visit. But don't expect a snack unless her mother, Helen, is away and Rhonda can find where the cookies or peanut butter is hidden.

Last year, Rhonda was diagnosed with Prader-Willi syndrome. The major symptom is an insatiable appetite. At only 4 feet, 9 inches tall, her frame is too small to carry her weight of

164 pounds. Her mother is glad to finally have a name for the disorder they've been fighting for years.

When Rhonda was born on Easter Sunday in 1956, her father went to church to pray that Rhonda might live. Because her muscles were unusually weak and floppy, doctors diagnosed Rhonda with brain damage and gave the Thompsons little hope that she would ever progress.

However, Rhonda surpassed their expectations. Only mildly developmentally delayed, she has no problem communicating or doing whatever she wants. In fact, that's part of the problem. Though Helen sometimes hides food or staples it closed, Rhonda is on to her tactics. As long as she can find the stapler, Rhonda simply opens the bag and eats, then makes sure it's again stapled shut securely when she's finished. Recently, Rhonda began to order an occasional pizza at night after her mom went to bed. She met the delivery person outside to prevent him from ringing the doorbell and waking her mother.

It's hard for Helen to be angry with Rhonda, who is sensitive and congenial. They lost their husband/father a few years ago. Two other children died with cystic fibrosis several years before that. But Helen and Rhonda cling to their faith and to each other.

Helen's greatest fear for Rhonda is that the extra weight on her small frame could cause heart failure, especially since she already suffers from sleep apnea. But according to Rhonda, the future is bright. She's visiting a dietitian, and every food in the house is fat free. She feels certain she will be successful at losing weight and even looks forward to a new group home that's in the planning stages for people with Prader-Willi syndrome.

But even if Rhonda moves away, mother and daughter will keep in constant touch and still travel together. They recently returned from a cruise with Richard Simmons on which they danced away a few pounds. But for Helen, travel is more than just enjoyable. "Take your child everywhere possible," says Helen. "Without realizing it, she gets a great education." Another piece of advice this mom would like to pass along is to "never underestimate what your child will achieve." After one visit with Rhonda, you'll have to agree!

A Christmas Miracle

Brian Vance is known at the local Wal-Mart for his smile and helpfulness. He works there as a greeter, and he also whizzes around the store in his motorized wheelchair, putting items back on shelves and doing any other job that needs to be done. Thirty-one at the time this is being written, Brian is extremely independent, living in his own apartment and taking care of his own needs. On weekends, he loves to fish and cruise around his parents' farm in his golf cart. But the road to independence was long.

At 13 years of age, Brian was injured in a hunting accident, which changed his life forever. A bullet entered his skull behind his left ear and lodged near his right eye. The injury damaged both sides of his brain, as well as the brain stem, and left him in a coma.

Doctors gave Brian little hope of survival. Six weeks later, with Brian still in a coma, his parents, Donna and Jack, were told their son would probably die soon from pneumonia or kidney failure. But they weren't convinced and stayed with him around the clock, talking to him, praying with him, and playing his favorite music and TV programs.

Since Brian had suffered no damage to his heart or lungs, a friend of Donna's who was a registered nurse encouraged them to exercise Brian's body. "We exercised anything that would move," says Donna, "starting with his thumb, wrist, and elbow, and eventually we worked on all his joints." Still in intensive care, Brian had multiple surgeries and suffered with uncontrollably high body temperatures and blood pressure. A shunt was placed in his brain to drain fluids, and a gasterostomy provided a permanent feeding tube.

Three months later, with his body temperature and blood pressure under control, Brian was moved to Children's Medical Center in Tulsa for intense therapy. Even though Brian was still in a coma and dependent on a feeding tube, Donna was determined to learn how to care for her son. "One of the aides helped me get past the fear of hurting Brian and taught me how to feed him," she says. By putting tiny amounts of a bland, creamy mixture into his mouth, then stroking his cheek and throat, she was able to get him to swallow. "I'm convinced that those feedings prevented paralysis and later allowed for speech," she concludes.

But three months of therapy brought only minor changes. Brian would sometimes open his eyes but would never track or follow an object. Finally, exhausted from the daily trips to the hospital and convinced that they could care for their son, the Vances asked to take Brian home.

"I wanted my family back together," says Donna, who had three other children at home. "The doctors were adamantly opposed to our taking him home, telling us to place him in a facility and go on with our lives. But I wasn't ready to give up on my son." The Vances believed that familiar surroundings and people who loved him would help Brian more than anything.

At home, the whole family rallied together, placing Brian in a lounge chair or bean bag chair in the living room, where there was lots of activity and laughter. His older sisters would sometimes place him in a wheelchair and push him around outside.

Another six weeks passed, and there was no noticeable change. It was now Christmas Eve, and Brian had been in a coma for seven and a half months. "We were at my mom's house," Donna says, "and we knew Brian was tired. He had been up all day with our family." Accustomed to talking to Brian, his dad placed him on the bed and said without thinking, "Brian, turn your head over."

In response, Brian actually turned his head!

Jack and Donna stared in shock but feared it was an isolated, automatic action. So Jack moved to the other side of the bed and said, "Brian, look over here." Brian again responded!

"It was the first time we were certain he was hearing us," says Donna. It was the miracle for which they had been praying.

Years of therapy followed before Brian was able to regain his speech or to move enough to be ambulatory. "It's not like the movies, where you just wake up and you're fine," says his mom. "It's a long, long process." But Brian's story has been an encouragement to others nonetheless. His doctors give hope to other parents by telling them of Brian's remarkable recovery, and Brian is quick to offer his testimony in the church his father pastors. "God was good to give us this miracle," says Donna. "But God is good no matter what happens. That's what's really important."

The Church Family

Unfortunately, many adults with special needs don't have the wonderful parents described above. Either their parents have already died, they live too far away, or they're just no longer a part of their children's lives. For these people, the church needs to come alongside and be their family. Whether they're members of our churches or simply residents in our communities, we can give them love, attention, and guidance.

Many disabled adults in group homes, intermediate-care facilities, and nursing homes have no voice in their own care or in what goes on around them. They may be exposed to negative behaviors, negligence, or even some form of abuse. The church may be the only Christian influence in their lives. We need to be positive spiritual role models. We need to be their friends. We need to be *Jesus* to them.

These individuals have great worth to God. If they were able to answer the question "What do you want to be now that you *are* grown up?" they would probably say, "I want to be loved, accepted, and treated with dignity." As God's special treasures, they deserve that and much more.

Encouragement from Scripture

- "Your strength will equal your days. . . . The eternal God is your refuge, and underneath are the everlasting arms" (Deuteronomy 33:25, 27).

- "I will give them a heart to know me, that I am the LORD. They will be my people, and I will be their God" (Jeremiah 24:7).

- "Now to each one the manifestation of the Spirit is given for the common good" (1 Corinthians 12:7).

- "And all of you serve each other with humble spirits, for God gives special blessings to those who are humble, but sets himself against those who are proud" (1 Peter 5:5, TLB).

CHAPTER 14

DEALING WITH PLACEMENT

Although some adults with special needs, like Scott and Doug in chapter 13, are ready to live in a group home, many families with younger children have to consider placement because of medical or other needs. Most parents hope they will be able to care for their disabled children at home and try heroically to provide for all their needs as long as they can. But in some cases, it becomes impossible.

Nancy and Steven Gray cared diligently and lovingly for their son Ben until he was two. Born with a rare chromosomal abnormality, he has seizures, severe respiratory problems, neurological impairments, visual and hearing impairment, psychomotor retardation, and a defective immune system. In addition, Ben's cognitive abilities are those of a two- to six-month-old baby.

Since Ben was sick almost all the time, his parents learned to do many day-to-day skilled nursing tasks and tricky medical procedures. In spite of various health crises, they managed his care at home for those two years. Since Steve's job frequently pulled him away from home, Ben's daily care fell on his mom's shoulders, and their other children, Kimberly and Christopher, got little attention. Ben's respiratory and immune systems were so fragile that in a matter of 20 minutes, he could go from being okay to being at death's door. A near-fatal reaction to one of his medications finally caused the Grays to decide to place their son in a 24-hours-a-day pediatric medical facility.

"The hardest thing is letting go and admitting you can't serve your child's needs yourself, and then turning over his care to someone else," Nancy says. She adds that people often think that placing your child is taking the easy way out, but it's just the opposite: "As stressful and difficult as it might be to care for a critically ill or total-care child at home, that's easier than the pain of letting go of control and trusting someone else with your child." Being unselfish enough to let go so the child's medical and/or educational needs can be met takes more strength, not less.

But while placing Ben at the Children's Center in Bethany, Oklahoma, was the hardest decision the Grays ever made, Ben has received such outstanding care that his health has actually improved. The center's special equipment and services are enabling Ben to have a much better quality of life with less serious illness.

The Breaking Point

When Lynn Becker's son Chris was eight years old, she consulted with his pediatrician about placing her son in a residential facility. Chris, who was nonverbal, had severe and profound retardation and autistic tendencies that caused him to self-abuse when upset. Being a former teacher, his mom had thrown herself into planning everything possible to help Chris. But now she was reaching her breaking point physically, mentally, and in her marriage.

As she and the doctor discussed the options, Lynn was told they would have a couple of years on a waiting list if they tried to place Chris, so they started the paperwork. Within six months, however, an opening came in a small Catholic group home with 35 children—the residence and school all in one building.

"It was so hard," says Lynn. "He was my firstborn, and I wasn't ready to relinquish him." Since the home is only a half hour from the family's house, however, they bring Chris home on weekends, and they visit him regularly. With his autistic tendencies, the routine and structure the school provides are beneficial, and Chris has thrived.

When Parents Seek Placement

Many factors lead parents to seek placement of their children in residential facilities. Single moms, for instance, must work full-time. Like Ben, some children have medical needs or behavioral problems their parents can't handle. And sometimes the parents get to the end of their rope, both physically and mentally, before placing a child. For a total-care child, the average age of placement is three years old.

"Often we see a family where marital problems are at the max, physical problems have begun, siblings may be having behavioral problems, and the mom's back is to the wall," says Barbara Youngblood, director of special services at the Children's Center for more than 18 years. Usually a combination of things has led to the placement decision; the parents know they can't keep all the pieces together.

One mother came into the center literally limping from the

physical toll of caring for her multihandicapped daughter for 24 hours a day over an eight-year period. Her child had a central line (an implanted IV line that allows medicine to be administered straight to the heart) and had to be lifted, diapered, and given IV fluids constantly. The mom had cared for her as long as she possibly could. "Hopefully," Barbara says, "parents can see the warning signs of exhaustion, depression, isolation of the family and child, the marriage in trouble, and personal health problems *before* there's a crisis."

Suggestions on Placement

The ideal situation is for a child to be cared for at home and his parents supplied all the physical, medical, and emotional support and services to handle both the child's and the siblings' needs. In some cases, that's possible. However, as Rosemarie S. Cook says, "If we lived in a perfect world, outside services would support all families who wanted to keep their children at home. Adequate home health care, respite services, tutoring, behavioral management, specialized equipment, recreation, vocational training, transportation, and finances would be provided. The real-world situation, however, is that at the same time that medical technology saves more special-needs babies, the public funding to provide services to those children is declining every year" (Parenting a Child with Special Needs *[Grand Rapids, Mich.: Zondervan, 1992], p. 170*).

When residential placement seems to be in the best interests of the child and family, therefore, here are some important things to consider:

1. To find the right place, first talk with your child's physicians, the special education department of the

school district, and the state department of education. State licensing agencies have lists of all the licensed centers and residential homes in the state. Also, talk with administrators at the local or regional children's hospitals, parent support groups, and organizations such as Easter Seals and United Cerebral Palsy.

2. There's nothing better than going and looking at facilities you're considering. Look at practical signs and symptoms: Are patients well cared for? Do they look good physically? Are they happy? When children are nutritionally well and cared for properly, they don't generally cry or whine. Constant whining or crying is usually caused by poor nutrition, children not being turned, dirty diapers, or being in a chair too long. What about cleanliness and the smells?

3. Go unannounced or on a weekend.

4. Check out what people think about the facility. Can you talk to a few families whose children are there? Call the city or county health department and ask what kind of inspection the facility had last. If there were deficiencies, were they healthcare or paperwork problems?

In addition, while you're considering facilities, begin to talk with extended family members and siblings about placement. Don't wait until you've already made the decision. Instead, invite a grandparent or special aunt who has been involved in the child's life to go along when you visit the home. Talk to your other children about what you're doing and why.

Questions to Ask

Although you can tell a great deal from touring the facility and looking around, you'll also want to ask some initial questions:

1. If you haven't already obtained this information, ask about their last Title 19 inspection and city/county inspection. Were there any deficiencies? If so, what were they?

2. Ask about payment: What kind of payment resources are available?

3. Ask about the credentials of the healthcare workers. Do they have registered physical therapists on staff? Do they have infant stimulation services? Are there one or more special education teachers on staff? Is a registered dietician watching calorie intake and making sure each patient gets adequate nutrition? Who's the physician, and how often does he see patients?

4. Concerning medication, is there a registered pharmacist who dispenses medication? Is medication given by a registered nurse, an assistant nurse, or an aide? (It's best if it's given by a registered nurse.)

5. Do they offer 24-hour nursing care? How many

nurses are on a shift? For medically fragile or total-care children, the night-shift staff is vital, so what's the ratio of patients to nurses in the night shift? in the day shift?

6. What are the policies for patient visits at home and family visits at the center?

(*Our thanks to Barbara Youngblood, director of special services at Children's Center, Bethany, Oklahoma, for her advice on placement and on the adjustment of parents and families to a child's living in a residential or medical center.*)

Adjusting to Your Child's Placement

When Sandy Rios got a call saying her daughter Sasha had been accepted at a residential care facility, she was speechless. Her daughter's care was getting more and more difficult, and after Sandy's divorce, the complications had increased. Her own back problems from years of lifting, plus her efforts to work full-time and support her family yet care for her disabled child, were becoming overwhelming. But it still broke her heart to have to stop being her daughter's primary caregiver. When the administrator said, "Sandy, we'll have a place for Sasha in two weeks," she burst out crying, mourning all over again.

Sandy had been Sasha's full-time caretaker for 20 years. For more than two years, she had also parented her 16-year-old son alone and tried to work. One of the ways she'd been able to cope that long was that once a month, her parents drove 300 miles to Chicago to help her for a week. Sasha's grandfather loves her deeply and hated to think about her not living at home. So when Sandy told him of Sasha's placement, he was upset.

However, Sandy's parents slowly began to see that this was God's timing and provision. "God opened the doors in a residential home because He knew what was around the corner," Sandy says. "Within a month after Sasha moved in at the home, my dad was diagnosed with cancer. Then he had to go through months of chemotherapy and treatment. And without my parents, I couldn't have managed."

Parents like Sandy experience a whole range of emotions when placing their child. As one dad said, "It wasn't an easy decision. We didn't want to admit we were helpless to take care of our child's growing medical needs."

Here are some ways you can help yourself and your family adjust when your child lives away from home:

1. Participate in a support group. Most facilities have such groups for parents. If your child's doesn't, start one. No one really understands what you're feeling and what you've been through except another family that's been through it. A support group is also a good way to find resources. The home may offer a grieving seminar or a class for siblings, too. As one mother says, "We never get out of the grieving cycle; it's like we're always grieving. There's the loss of what our child could have been. And every time he gets in trouble medically or anything else, we begin to grieve all over again and think, *This may be the time he dies.* We need to be able to express and work through those feelings."

2. Try to connect all the family members and give them opportunities to talk about how they feel. For grandparents, for example, it's a double pain because they're grieving for their child *and* grandchild. Also, husbands and wives need to keep communicating.

3. Help siblings express feelings. They often get lost in the whole process, and no one is listening to how they feel about their sister or brother's being placed in a residential home. Siblings also feel a lot of guilt. Younger children may not know why the disability happened and wonder if it will happen to them. They may be experiencing anger and grief as well.

4. Most important, remain involved with your child. When parents stay away from a child who has been placed because they find visiting the home too painful, they don't heal and their child suffers from their absence. Maintaining closeness is healthy for both the disabled child and the whole family. To remain involved, try the following:

- Visit as regularly as you can considering distance, job, and other children and responsibilities.

- Take your child home for weekend and holiday visits, for an hour at a time, or for whatever period you can so your child remains an important, valid part of the family. Giving siblings the ongoing opportunity to interact is vital.

- Participate in family activities sponsored by the residential home. Even centers for multihandicapped and medically fragile children have family picnics, family photo days, and opportunities for parents to accompany the kids on trips to the Ice Capades, circus, zoo, and so on.

• Start to think long term rather than short term. Help your child by taking care of yourself so you'll be there to love and support her and supervise her care over the long haul. Get a lot of rest.

• Enjoy family holidays and your spouse, friends, and other children. It's hard to let go and begin to live, and sometimes you don't feel you have the right to be happy. If you've been caring for a total-care child, you may have forgotten what you used to like to do. Think back to what you enjoyed doing or have always wanted to try: a hobby, a part-time job, a craft, a ministry, or a talent you want to develop.

• Drop in at the residential home frequently, and never at the same time twice in a row, especially if your child is a total-care patient. The time most critical to visit initially is weekends (when staffing is generally lower). Then the nursing staff begins to know you're visible and involved, and your child will get better-than-average care.

• Avoid relinquishing your rights as a parent. When the Beckers placed their son Chris in a group home, they were told they had to give up their parental rights and he had to be made a ward of the state. "It's easier to handle paperwork if the child is a ward of the state, so parents considering placement are often told that," says Lynn.

The truth, however, is that you don't have to give up custody. "We're Chris's guardians and are involved in decisions no matter where he's placed," Lynn affirms. "Don't sign away your rights to your child!" At 20 years old as we write this, Chris is now in a group home with seven young adults about 30 minutes from the family house in Colorado Springs. He can stay there until he's 21; then his parents will have to find adult placement. They have remained fully involved in his health care and education and have orders on file that before he is given any medical procedures, flu shots, or blood tests, they have to be notified and grant their permission.

Just the Right Place

By no means are all stories about special-needs children being placed in a residential home sad. When Sarah Reynolds was in high school, for example, she began to talk about "going away" to live just like all the other girls in her Bible study at church. As they made their plans for college, Sarah asked her mom to help her look into group homes. Sarah had cerebral palsy but a very independent spirit!

Sarah's preparation for graduating to more independent living actually started many years before. By kindergarten, she was partially mainstreamed. In junior high, she was in a special ed class part of the day and mainstreamed in other courses. In high school, she was in special education half the day and in a work/study program that included a job in the school cafeteria. She also attended a vocational-technical college for occupational training, a good springboard for being employable. After having her first real job, Sarah felt she was ready to launch.

Following much prayer and searching for the right place, plus two years on the waiting list after she was accepted, Sarah moved into the Center of Family Love, approximately 30 miles from her family. After her initial week of homesickness, Sarah felt happy and at home. She loves her weekends home but is always ready to go back.

"She has friends, a good job, and a life there," says her mom, Susie. "She considers it her home away from home!"

An Ending Becomes a Beginning

When Ben Scott was first diagnosed with autism, the doctors' theory was that "Mommy did it." They thought he had retreated from reality because he felt unloved. Shattered by this news, Carole, his mother, had to work hard not to give in to severe depression. "I knew it wasn't true," she says, "but I was young and vulnerable and thought the doctors were specialists."

Ben had developed normally until the age of two and a half, learning to walk and talk, even in sentences. But then he began to regress. He stuttered, then stopped talking, then replaced his normal speech pattern with "echolalia"—repeating what was said to him. "He related and perceived things so differently as a child that I was very fearful of the future for him—of how he would fit into the world's scheme of things," Carole says. "He seemed to have such potential, yet he was off in another world. Ben was a very normal-looking young man bound up in a body that couldn't communicate."

Never a "cuddly" child, Ben began to have outbursts of rage, which became increasingly difficult to control. Carole and her husband gradually accepted the fact that Ben would no longer be able to live at home, and when he was 13 they moved him into a facility that could better meet his needs. In spite of a *peace* in knowing this was best for Ben, parting was painful.

"When he went away, it was like a death in the family, yet there was no rite of passage to help us through it," Carole reports. "There was no funeral, no one coming with food, no cards, and no one knew what to say. You feel so alone, and you grieve as if it really were a death. For me, all hope just went out the window."

Then a friend invited Carole to a Christian women's club luncheon. At that event, she asked Jesus into her heart. Soon after that, her husband also became a Christian.

"It was the only way we could handle the pain," says Carole. "It was as if God wrapped me in a cocoon of peace and love." Carole began to study her Bible and found Romans 8:28: "And we know that in all things God works for the good of those who love him, who have been called according to his purpose."

"The *good* was that my husband and I came to know Jesus when Ben moved away, and that at age 34, Ben is happier than he has ever been in his life," says Carole today. When he's home on visits, Ben loves to go to church. He also listens to Christian music and even prays with Carole. He has a pleasant countenance now and projects joy to others, a stark contrast to his childhood. And at the end of a home visit, Ben always gives his mom a special hug.

"When Ben was younger, my husband once said, 'Maybe he will be your comfort in your old age.' I couldn't imagine it then," Carole says. "But now Ben has become more than a comfort. He is truly a kindred spirit! What I thought was an *ending* actually became a *beginning*."

Letting Go

Pam Whitley has a photo of her daughter Jan from when she first went into the Children's Center several years ago, and now there's no comparison. Today Jan is bubbly, happier, and healthier. Although her parents know that placing her there was the right decision and that her quality of life has improved so much because of the 24-hour-a-day skilled care and special equipment, monitors, and oxygen, letting go was still extremely painful.

Pam had been committed to taking care of Jan forever and had prayed that she could. But in spite of Pam's devoted care, Jan's breathing problems worsened, and her overall health was rapidly deteriorating. So was her mother's.

"In my mother's heart, I'd already decided what was best for Jan—for me to take care of her the rest of her life," Pam says. "But there comes a time when you need to pray, 'Thy will be done, and show me, Lord,' and trust that God knows what's best for your child."

Every case and every child's needs are unique. Some families live next door to grandparents or have a big family as a support system. But the Whitleys didn't have that help. And finding an individual to help wouldn't work either—Pam needed a whole staff when Jan's medical needs got greater and her own strength was dwindling.

Although she visited her daughter every day after the placement, when she would walk away from the center, Pam had to talk to herself about why Jan was there. She recognized that life brings seasons of change and that if she ruined her own health, she couldn't watch over Jan's life. She also had to choose to trust God with Jan's life and care.

"I choose to believe Psalm 91 is true for Jan—that God will

give His angels watch over her—and also that just because Jan is handicapped, Jeremiah 29:11 isn't negated for her. God still does have a future and a hope for her. He isn't through with Jan yet—He's still doing a work!"

Encouragement From Scripture

- "For he will command his angels concerning you to guard you in all your ways" (Psalm 91:11).

- "Take tender care of those who are weak" (1 Thessalonians 5:14, TLB).

- "He heals the brokenhearted and binds up their wounds" (Psalm 147:3).

- "Since the Lord is directing our steps, why try to understand everything that happens along the way?" (Proverbs 20:24, TLB).

- "For I am the Lord your God, the holy one of Israel, your Savior" (Isaiah 43:3).

AFTERWORD

Like a much-loved hymn with verses yet to be sung, many wonderful stories still wait to be told, making it difficult to end this book. When we started this project, we had no idea how many people would touch our lives and warm our hearts with their words of hope, heartache, life, love, and perseverance.

Although the challenges and family situations differed, each story carried a central theme—God is faithful! God is sovereign! When you can't see the light at the end of the tunnel, you just grab hold of God's hand and keep walking. He knows the way. When we can't understand everything or answer all the whys, we can trust His character and His heart toward us. He knows our needs, our pain, and our joy. Romans 8:28 holds true: "And we know that in all things God works for the good of those who love him, who have been called according to his purpose." What hope that verse holds for parents of children with special needs! God *can* and *does* bring good from all situations. We may not understand the reason for a disability, but we know God will use it for His glory.

We're thankful for the many "challenged" families who opened their hearts to us and invited us into the most intimate part of their souls. Then they wrapped us in their prayers while we wrote, with the hope of helping other parents who might one day walk the path they're now traveling. They whispered prayers as they drove to endless therapies, hooked up feeding tubes, struggled with IEPs, and waited countless hours in doctors' offices or hospital rooms. Even as they fixed braces, wheelchairs, and head wands or kissed their sleeping children, they remembered us in prayer. They are the heroes of this book—the moms, the dads, and the children with special needs.

From the beginning of this writing, we believed we were sharing a part of God's heart with you. We still feel that way. We're honored and humbled that God used us to tell the stories of "extra-ordinary" parents and children who go about their lives every day without complaint, never allowing a disability to steal their joy. Even in the midst of pain or ridicule, they open their hearts and arms to everyone—even strangers. They've inspired us with their faith and tenacity and are running the race set before them with patience and even joy.

Still, there are times when people with disabilities are not received well by others, and we hurt for them when this happens. But in heaven, their homecoming will be one of reward and glorious victory. What a brilliant crown they will receive from their heavenly Father as they hear, "Well done, good and faithful servant!" (Matthew 25:21). We pray that your heart has been encouraged by these testimonies of faith and that Jesus Christ has been magnified and glorified.

Resources

Organizations

National organizations and associations are valuable supports for families of children with special needs. They work to improve the lives of people with a specific disability, support research, develop educational materials, and hold regional and national conferences. National organizations also work with local support groups and medical and educational professionals. They have articles, cassette tapes, and videos for loan or purchase. They provide information on up-to-date educational strategies and medical treatment and can connect you to other resources, technology, and services.

Alexander Graham Bell Association for the Deaf
3417 Volta Place NW

Washington, DC 20007
(202) 337–5220
E–mail: agbell2@aol.com
URL: http://www.agbell.org

Alliance of Genetic Support Groups
35 Wisconsin Circle, Suite 440
Chevy Chase, MD 20815
(800) 336–4363; (301) 652–5553
E–mail: alliance@capaccess.org
URL: http://medhlp.netusa.net/www/agsg.htm

American Foundation for the Blind (AFB)
11 Penn Plaza, Suite 300
New York, NY 10001
(800) 232–5463
(212) 502–6700; (212) 502–7662
E–mail: afbinfo@afb.org
URL: http://www.afb.org/afb

American Speech–Language–Hearing Association
(ASHA)
10801 Rockville Pike
Rockville, MD 20852
(800) 638–8255; (301) 897–5700
E–mail: webmaster@asha.org
URL: http://www2.asha.org/asha

Association for the Care of Children's Health (ACCH)
7910 Woodmont Avenue, Suite 300
Bethesda, MD 20814–3015
(301) 654–6549; (800) 808–2224

E–mail: acch@acch.org
URL: http://www.wsd.com/acch.org

Association for Persons with Severe Handicaps (TASH)
29 W. Susquehanna Avenue, Suite 210
Baltimore, MD 21204
(410) 828–8274; (410) 828–1306
E–mail: info@tash.org

The ARC (formerly the Association for Retarded
Citizens)
500 East Border Street, Suite 300
Arlington, TX 76010
(800) 433–5255; (817) 261–6003; (817) 277–0553
E–mail: tharc@metronet.com
URL: http://thearc.org/welcome.html

Autism Society of America
7910 Woodmont Avenue, Suite 650
Bethesda, MD 20814–3015
(800) 3–AUTISM; (301) 657–0881
URL: http://www.autism–society.org

Beach Center on Families and Disability
3111 Haworth Hall
University of Kansas
Lawrence, KS 66045
(913) 864–7600
FAX: (913) 864–7605
E–mail: beach@dole.lalukans.edu

Children and Adults with Attention Deficit Disorders (CH.A.D.D.)
499 NW 70th Avenue, Suite 101
Plantation, FL 33317
(800) 233–4050; (954) 587–3700
URL: http://www.chadd.org

Council for Exceptional Children (CEC)
1920 Association Drive
Reston, VA 20190–1589
(703) 620–3660; (703) 264–9446
E–mail: cec@cec.sped.org
URL: http://www.cec.sped.org/home.htm

Cystic Fibrosis Foundation
6931 Arlington Road
Bethesda, MD 20814
(800)344–4823
URL: www.cff.org

Direct Link for the Disabled, Inc.
P. O. Box 1036
Solvang, CA 93464
(805) 688–1603
A link to available resources for all disabilities, health conditions, and rare disorders. Over 38 resource packets available with complete information about disorder, national organizations to contact, fact sheets, sources for further reading, and so on. Newsletter, research, health information, hotlinks to other sites through their home page on the Internet: www.directlinkup.com.

Epilepsy Foundation of America (EFA)
4351 Garden City Drive, 5th Floor
Landover, MD 20785–4941
(800) 332–1000; (301) 459–3700
E–mail: postmaster@efa.org
URL: http://www.efa.org

Family Resource Center on Disabilities
20 East Jackson Blvd., Room 900
Chicago, IL 60604
(800) 952–4199; (312) 939–3513; (312) 939–3519

Friendship Foundation/Friendship Ministries
2850 Kalamazoo Avenue SE
Grand Rapids, MI 49560
(606) 241–1691; (800) 333–8300
or P. O. Box 5070
Burlington, ON L7R3Y8   Canada
(800) 263–4252
   This ministry offers religious educational curricula
and provides assistance to churches to reach and teach
people with mental disabilities.

International Resource Center for Down Syndrome
Keith Building
2323 South Sheppard, Suite 1000
Houston, TX 77019
(713) 520–0232; (713) 520–5136
E–mail: ilru@bcm.tmc.edu
URL: http://www.bcm.tmc.edu/ilru

International Rett Syndrome Association
9121 Piscataway Road, Suite 2B
Clinton, MD 20735–2561
(800) 818–7388; (301) 856–3334
E–mail: irsa@paltech.com
URL: http://www2.paltech.com/irsa/irsa.htm

JAF Ministries
The Disability Outreach of Joni Eareckson Tada
P. O. Box 3333
Agoura Hills, CA 91301
(818) 707–5664
    JAF Ministries offers many printed resources and
retreats for families with a member who is disabled. Check
with JAF Ministries for the states in which the retreats are
being held each summer.

Learning Disability Association of America (LDA)
4156 Library Road
Pittsburgh, PA 15234
(412) 341–1515; (412) 341–8077

Muscular Dystrophy Association (MDA)
3300 East Sunrise Drive
Tucson, AZ 85718
(520) 529–2000
E–mail: mda@mdausa.org
URL: http://www.mdausa.org

National Association of Protection and Advocacy
Systems
900 Second Street NE, Suite 211

Washington, DC 20002
(202) 408–9514; (202) 408–9521
E–mail: hn4537@handsnet.org

National Down Syndrome Congress
1605 Chantilly Drive, Suite 250
Atlanta, GA 30324
(800) 232–6372; (404) 633–1555
E–mail: ndsc@charitiesusa.com

National Easter Seal Society, Inc.
230 West Monroe Street, Suite 1800
Chicago, IL 60606
(800) 221–6827; (312) 726–6200; (312) 726–4258
E–mail: nassinfo@seals.com
URL: http://www.seals.com

National Fragile X Foundation
1441 York Street, Suite 303
Denver, CO 80206
(800) 688–8765; (303) 333–6155

National Information Center for Children and Youth with
Disabilities (NICHCY)
P. O. Box 1492
Washington, DC 20013-1492
(800) 695-0285
E-mail: nichcy@aed.org
World wide web: http://www.aed.org/nichcy

National Library Services for the Blind & Physically Handicapped
The Library of Congress
Washington, DC 20542
(800) 424–8567; (800) 424–9100; (202) 707–5100
E–mail: nls@loc.gov
URL: http://www.loc.gov/nls

National Parent Network on Disabilities
1600 Prince Street, #115
Alexandria, VA 22314
(703) 684–6763
FAX: (703) 836–1232

Orton Dyslexia Society
Chester Building #382
8600 LaSalle Road
Baltimore, MD 21286–2044
(800) 222–3123; (410) 296–0232
E–mail: ods@pieorg
URL: http://www.ods.org

Parents Helping Parents: The Parent–Directed Family Resource Center for Children with Special Needs
3041 Olcott Street
Santa Clara, CA 95054
(408) 727–5775
E–mail: info@php.com
URL: http://www.php.com

Project DOCC (Delivery of Chronic Care)
(516) 365-0959
    This program works with medical schools and

young pediatricians to help them understand just how much they can and should do for the chronically ill child and family.

Recording for the Blind and Dyslexic
The Anne T. Macdonald Center
20 Roszel Road
Princeton, NJ 08540
(800) 221–4793; (609) 452–0606
URL: http://www.rfb.org

Sibling Support Project/National Association of Sibling Programs (NASP)
Children's Hospital and Medical Center
4800 Sand Point Way, NE
P. O. Box 5372 CL–09
Seattle, WA 98105–0371
(206) 368–4912
FAX: (206) 368–4816 (ask for newsletter)

Special Olympics International
1325 G Street NW, Suite 500
Washington, DC 20005
(202) 628–3630
URL: http://www.specialolympics.org/

Spina Bifida Association of America
4590 MacArthur Blvd. NW, Suite 250
Washington, DC 20007–4226
(800) 621–3141; (202) 944–3285
E–mail: spinabifida@aol.com
URL: http://www.infohiway.com/spinabifida

Tourette Syndrome Association
42–40 Bell Boulevard
Bayside, NY 11361
(718) 224–2999

United Cerebral Palsy Association, Inc.
1660 L Street, Suite 700
Washington, DC 20036
(202) 776–0406; (800) 872–5827
E–mail: ucpnatl@ucpa.org
URL: http://www.ucpa.org

Williams Syndrome Association
1312 N. Campbell, Suite 33
Royal Oak, MI 48067
(810) 541–3630
FAX: (810) 541–3631

Publications

Exceptional Parent
605 Commonwealth Avenue
Boston, MA 02215
(800) 247–8080; (800) 562–1973
URL: http://www.familyeducation.com

*NATHHAN (National Challenged Homeschoolers Assoc.
Network) Magazine*
5383 Alpine Road SE
Olalla, WA 98359
(206) 857–4257

FAX: (206) 857–7764
E–mail: NATHANEWS@aol.com

Sibling Information Network Newsletter
University of Connecticut
249 Glenbrook Road, Box U–64
Storrs, CT 06269–2064
(860) 486–4985
FAX: (860) 486–5037

Special Education Today
127 Ninth Avenue North
Nashville, TN 37234
(800) 458–2772

Special Family: Restoring Hope to Families with Special Needs
P. O. Box 15412
Irving, TX 75015–4512
(214) 256–8014

Note: Most of the national associations for specific disabilities have their own newsletter or magazine, which you can order from the organization address listed above.

Recommended Books and Other Resources

James Dobson, *When God Doesn't Make Sense* (Tyndale, 1993).

Joni Eareckson Tada, *Joni* (Zondervan, 1977).

Joni Eareckson Tada, *Glorious Intruder* (Zondervan, 1994).

Joni Eareckson Tada, *Heaven* (Zondervan, 1995).

Cheri Fuller, *Trading Your Worry for Wonder* (Broadman & Holman, 1996). This book is a comprehensive guide for women on overcoming anxiety and fear.

Cheri Fuller, *When Mothers Pray* (Multnomah, 1997). A guide to praying for your children and overcoming hindrances to prayer.

Gallaudet University Press, *The Comprehensive Signed English Dictionary*, 800 Florida Avenue NE, Washington, DC 20002–3695; (202) 651–5488.

Include Us, a delightful video for ages 2 to 12 that helps "typical" children know they can be friends with those who have special needs, and helps disabled kids realize they aren't really different from other children. Available at many Blockbuster video stores, by calling (888) 462–5833, or online at http:\\IncludeUs.com.

D. J. Lobato, *Brothers, Sisters, and Special Needs: Information and Activities for Helping Young Siblings of Children with Chronic Illnesses and Developmental Disabilities* (Paul H. Brookes Publishing, [800] 638–3775).

Dr. Grant Martin, *Help! My Child Isn't Learning* (Focus on the Family, 1995). A comprehensive guide for any school problems and learning disabilities, including attention deficit disorder and dyslexia.

Fern Nichols, *Moms in Touch International: Mothers Meeting to Pray for Their Children & Schools* (MITI, P. O. Box 1120, Poway, CA 92074-1120, [619] 486–4065; also available at Christian bookstores). This book tells how to start a Moms in Touch group for your children's school, and how to pray scripturally and in one accord.

People's Medical Society, *Dial 800 for Health.* Contains more than 80,000 toll–free numbers nationwide for health problems and disabilities, from stroke, surgery services, and Tourette syndrome to cerebral palsy, genetic disorders, vision impairments, and more.

Marilyn Phillips, *A Cheerleader for Life* (Rejoice Publishing, P. O. Box 14763, Ft. Worth, TX 76117). The true story of the author's daughter Rebekah and their triumph over the effects of cystic fibrosis.

Pam Whitley, *Not a Glimmer of Hope: Learning to Follow the Shepherd When the Path Seems Impossible*

(Send the Light Ministries, 7230 NW 105 Terrace, Oklahoma City, OK 73162; [405] 728–0507).

Norm Wright, *Crisis Care,* a series of nine videos and workbook to train the average layperson in how to minister to other people when they're hurting (Grace Products); and *Recovering from the Losses of Life* (Revell), with curriculum to teach groups. Both are available from Christian Marriage Enrichment, 17821 17th Street, Suite 190, Tustin, CA 92780; (800) 875–7560.

Norm and Joyce Wright, *I'll Love You Forever: Accepting Your Child When Your Expectations Are Unfulfilled* (Focus on the Family, 1993).